T0013318

Money in the Light of Eternity

MONEY IN THE
LIGHT OF ETERNITY

What the Bible Says about
Your Financial Purpose

ART RAINER

TYNDALE
MOMENTUM®

A Tyndale nonfiction imprint

Visit Tyndale online at tyndale.com.

Visit Tyndale Momentum online at tyndalemomentum.com.

Tyndale, Tyndale's quill logo, *Tyndale Momentum*, and the Tyndale Momentum logo are registered trademarks of Tyndale House Ministries. Tyndale Momentum is a nonfiction imprint of Tyndale House Publishers, Carol Stream, Illinois.

Money in the Light of Eternity: What the Bible Says about Your Financial Purpose

Copyright © 2023 by Church Answers. All rights reserved.

Cover illustration of infinity symbol copyright © Alhovik/Shutterstock. All rights reserved.

Cover design by Faceout Studio, Spencer Fuller

Unless otherwise indicated, all Scripture quotations are taken from the *Holy Bible*, New Living Translation, copyright © 1996, 2004, 2015 by Tyndale House Foundation. Used by permission of Tyndale House Publishers, Carol Stream, Illinois 60188. All rights reserved.

Scripture quotations marked CSB are taken from the Christian Standard Bible,® copyright © 2017 by Holman Bible Publishers. Used by permission. Christian Standard Bible® and CSB® are federally registered trademarks of Holman Bible Publishers.

Scripture quotations marked NIV are taken from the Holy Bible, New International Version,® NIV.® Copyright © 1973, 1978, 1984, 2011 by Biblica, Inc.® Used by permission. All rights reserved worldwide.

For information about special discounts for bulk purchases, please contact Tyndale House Publishers at csresponse@tyndale.com, or call 1-855-277-9400.

Library of Congress Cataloging-in-Publication Data

A catalog record for this book is available from the Library of Congress.

ISBN 978-1-4964-7376-9

Printed in China

29	28	27	26	25	24	23
7	6	5	4	3	2	1

To Chuck and Pam Lawless,
Thank you for loving our family.
Thank you for living generously.

CONTENTS

PREPARING YOUR HEART
FOR ETERNITY

Too often in the church, when the conversation turns to money or generosity, we're tempted to run and hide. We feel as if someone is trying to pick our pockets. We want to avoid the implied judgment that seems to go along with discussions about finances, so we shut down.

Let me put your mind at ease: This book is not about taking something from you. My sole purpose in writing this is to give you a very significant, life-changing gift.

God doesn't want your money. He wants your heart. And your heart deeply desires God and the good gifts that come from him alone. It's the way we're wired.

Your heart has profound longings. It longs for contentment. It longs for satisfaction. It longs for happiness. It longs for you to be part of something greater than yourself. You feel these desires and longings as you go through life. You cannot shake them. They're part of being human.

Let's be honest: You know that money plays an important role in life and that what you do with your money matters. Maybe you've tried to satisfy your heart's longings by seeking after more money and more stuff. But now you realize it's like junk food—full of quickly fading satisfaction that leaves you unhealthier than you were before.

What if I could show you that God's plan for *every* area of your life—including money—will lead you to greater contentment, greater satisfaction, greater joy, and greater significance in your life?

If you align yourself with that plan, it will prepare your heart for eternity.

Does your heart long to be content? God wants to give you contentment.

Does your heart long to be satisfied? God wants to give you satisfaction.

Does your heart long for happiness? God wants to give you joy.

Does your heart long to be a part of something greater than yourself? God's most ambitious mission is ready for you to join.

When was the last time you used money in a way that brought about deep, refreshing joy and satisfaction—for yourself and others? God uses money in your life not so you can build up a heavenly money market account, but to mold your heart into one that looks more like his. When you follow God's design for your life, you will find what no large bank account, big house, or fast car could ever provide. You will find your true heart.

This book is ultimately about your heart and what it truly means to be generous.

1

LIVING FOR SOMETHING
GREATER THAN YOURSELF

He went after that high-paying job, sacrificing much, and now he's acquired it.

He dreamed of living in that big house in the upscale part of town, and now he owns it.

He desired to travel to exotic locations around the world, and now he's been there.

He used to imagine himself behind the wheel of that expensive car, and now he drives it.

He wanted a full bank account and a financially secure retirement, and now he has it.

He has a lot.

But if you caught him in a moment of honesty, he would tell you that sometimes it feels like he has nothing. He would tell you that he regularly looks at his possessions and feels empty, even lost. He tries to push those feelings aside, but it doesn't work. He's frustrated by how this has all turned out. Though he has lived for himself his entire adult life, it is precisely his *self* that somehow feels neglected.

His heart feels ignored.

Though he is a Christian and regularly attends church, he has never really been involved there, especially with his pocketbook. He hasn't given much from his resources over the years. It isn't that he doesn't trust the church to use the money well, it's that he has put his own trust in money—for hope, happiness, contentment, and security in life. So he has held on tightly to what he has.

Yet, it seems the tighter he holds on to his possessions, the looser his grip becomes on a life that matters.

He knows some people who do things differently. In fact, there are several in the church he attends. They don't live in the same type of house, drive the same type of car, or make the same type of salary, yet they act as if they have more.

They seem genuinely content. And happy.

Maybe these people are just faking it. Maybe they aren't really that content. But their consistency, week after week, month after month, and year after year makes him question his perception.

Maybe they're the real deal. Maybe they know something he doesn't.

There's definitely something different about those church members.

DESIGNED FOR GENEROSITY

Researchers have completed several studies on the relationship between generosity and happiness.

In one study, a group of adults was asked to rate their level of happiness in the morning.[1] Afterward, they were given an envelope containing either five dollars or twenty dollars, along with one of two instructions for the day.

Some were told to use the money for themselves—to pay a personal bill, buy themselves a cup of coffee, or whatever self-focused spending they preferred. Others were told to use the money for someone else—to purchase someone's food, pay their bill, or perform some other generous act.

The participants followed the instructions. During the day, some used the money to benefit themselves, and some used the money to benefit others. Later that evening, they were again asked to rate their level of happiness.

Those who used the money for someone else reported higher levels of happiness than those who used the money for themselves. Generosity produced higher levels of happiness than self-focused spending.

These results are not uncommon. Regardless of demographics, other studies have produced similar results.

In another study, individuals in Canada and South Africa were provided with the money needed to purchase a small goody bag.[2] Like the participants in the previous study, recipients rated their initial happiness level and were given one of two instructions. One group was told to purchase a goody bag for themselves. The second group was instructed to purchase a goody bag for a sick child at a local hospital.

At the end of the day, the participants were again asked to rate their level of happiness. The results likely won't surprise you. Those who purchased goody bags for a sick child reported higher happiness levels than those who purchased a goody bag for themselves. The outcome was consistent in both Canada and South Africa.

Studies like these remind us of what the Bible has been telling us all along: God is a generous God, and he has designed us for generosity, to reflect his character. In other words, God calls us to live and give generously because generosity aligns with our design.

We are made in God's image. And though sin has distorted this image, it has not destroyed it. God is glad to be generous, and when we give, we experience gladness as well.

Intuitively, you already know this. Your heart tells you.

Recall the last time you gave sacrificially. Did you give to your local church? Did you provide funds for a homeless shelter? Did you provide backpacks and school supplies for families who could not afford them? Did you financially support mission work in another country?

How do you think about that generosity right now? The memory likely brings back feelings of happiness or satisfaction—certainly not regret. Though we often regret past purchases, we rarely regret past generosity.

You were meant for more than a big house, fast car, nice vacation, and full bank account. You were meant for something far more significant and satisfying than tending to your own needs.

God designed you and me for generosity.

ONE OR THE OTHER

In the Gospel of Mark, we are introduced to a man who is often called the rich young ruler. He comes to Jesus seeking the path to eternal life. After the man insists that he has kept the Ten Commandments since his youth, Jesus says to him, "There is still one thing you haven't done. . . . Go and sell all your possessions and give the money to the poor, and you will have treasure in heaven. Then come, follow me" (Mark 10:21).

Mark then adds, "At this the man's face fell, and he went away sad, for he had many possessions" (Mark 10:22).

An idol is anything we devote ourselves to or rely upon that is not God. This man wanted an earthly life marked by accumulating possessions, *and* he wanted eternal life in the end.

Like so many in our day, he was trying to love God *and* money—which is something Jesus taught is not possible.

"No one can serve two masters. For you will hate one and love the other; you will be devoted to one and despise the other. You cannot serve God and be enslaved to money" (Matthew 6:24).

Jesus knew not only how this rich man's heart worked, but how every human heart works. A heart consumed with the desire for money and possessions cannot be simultaneously consumed with a desire for Jesus. One love must win out.

You may wonder why Jesus asked the rich man to give up everything. Simply stated, Jesus wanted to *give* him everything, which requires open hands. Following Jesus means being ready to do what he wants us to do and to go where he wants us to go. Hands clutching earthly riches will never be able to hold tightly to Jesus and the treasure that comes with following him.

The question is this: *Are you willing to let go?* God may not prompt you to give away every earthly possession, but are you willing to hold loosely the things of this world so that you can fully grasp the things of God?

Sadly, the rich man looked down at the ground, turned around, and walked away.

Let me encourage you to make a different decision and live paradoxically.

THE PARADOX

From a global perspective, most Americans are considered rich. Compared to those immediately around you, you might not *feel* rich, but those feelings are deceiving. You have more resources right now than most people in the world will acquire in their lifetime. In terms of global wealth, you are the rich young ruler.

In 1 Timothy 6:17-19, Paul instructs Timothy what to tell those who are considered rich in this world.

Teach those who are rich in this world not to be proud and not to trust in their money, which is so unreliable. Their trust should be in God, who richly gives us all we need for our enjoyment. Tell them to use their money to do good. They should be rich in good works and generous to those in need, always being ready to share with others. By doing this they will be storing up their treasure as a good foundation for the future so that they may experience true life.

Even if we have great financial resources, we are not to place our hope in money. Money is guaranteed to disappoint. Instead, we are to place our trust in God and be generous with what he has granted us.

The result of such generosity?

True life.

True life is not found in the acquiring of things, but in the sharing of things.

True life is genuine contentment. True life is lasting satisfaction. True life is knowing we are part of something larger than ourselves. True life is joy.

But if we want to experience true life, we must first *let go*.

It's a paradox.

Hold loosely to money. Hold loosely to bank accounts. Hold loosely to cars. Hold loosely to houses. Hold loosely to vacations. Hold loosely to everything so you may hold tightly to true life.

Deep inside, you already know this. You were created for something more. Your possessions were entrusted to you for something greater than your own comfort and security.

The rich young ruler walked away disappointed. Those who follow Paul's teaching in 1 Timothy 6 will taste true life. There will be no disappointment for them.

CREATED FOR SOMETHING MORE

You know you were created for something more—more than a high-paying job, more than a big house, more than an expensive car, more than exotic vacations, and more than a fully funded retirement account.

You're not surprised when you run into people who seem to have it all on the outside but are empty and unsatisfied on the inside. Maybe at this moment you're one of them.

God designed us to live in a paradox. We may have much or we may have little, but with everything we are to be open-handed, ready to give freely and abundantly. When we hold our possessions loosely, we are able to grasp true life. It is then that we find ourselves fully engaged, contented, and on an adventure we never could have scripted. No matter the extent of your resources, you and your money were designed for eternity-shaping generosity.

WHERE DO YOU GO FROM HERE?

1. Read Mark 10:21-22. What are three ways that you have found yourself acting like the rich young ruler?

2. When was the last time a purchase made you feel deep, lasting satisfaction and contentment?

3. Read 1 Timothy 6:17-19 in light of the research discussed in this chapter. Why do you think generosity produces a greater sense of happiness?

4. Pray that God will give you the courage to let go of the things of this world so that you may grasp true life.

2

SHAPING ETERNITY

Have you ever read a book that had a profound impact on the way you view your life? For me, it was the introduction in a book called *Inheritolatry* by James D. Wise. It's a slender volume about creating a positive financial legacy that will have an eternal impact—by how we designate the use of our financial resources when we die.

Over the next thirty years or so, an estimated $30 trillion will pass from one generation of Americans to the next through inheritances. It has been called the "great wealth transfer."[3] Wise estimates that $5 trillion "of God's money . . . has been entrusted to this generation of Christians,"[4] and that "completing the work of the Great Commission can be accomplished . . . by simply applying God's principles of inheritance to the estate planning and wealth transfer process."[5]

According to some mission organizations, there are approximately 3,200 unreached and unengaged people groups in the world. These are people who have yet to hear the name of Jesus. They have not yet been given the opportunity to know the hope we have.

Based on Wise's numbers, it takes $75,000 per year to reach one unreached people group. Truly engaging a group takes time. Let's assume it takes twenty years to fully engage with a people group.

Here's the math:

3,200 people groups x $75,000 per year x 20 years = $4.8 billion

Now look at that $4.8 billion in light of the $5 trillion that American Christians may receive through inheritances alone.

One trillion equals one thousand billion. The amount needed is a drop in the bucket when compared to the amount available.

You can analyze and adjust the numbers all you want. The fact remains that we have the resources to reach every tongue, tribe, and nation in our generation.

Right before Jesus ascended to heaven, he gave his disciples this command:

Therefore, go and make disciples of all the nations,
baptizing them in the name of the Father and the
Son and the Holy Spirit. Teach these new disciples
to obey all the commands I have given you. And be
sure of this: I am with you always, even to the end
of the age.

MATTHEW 28:19-20

This is known as the Great Commission. And we have
the resources to do it.

In our lifetime.

I often wonder, *What if we don't?* Knowing what we
know. Having the resources we have. What if we don't do
anything about it? What if we sit on the sidelines, watching
the opportunity pass our generation by?

What will future generations of believers think of us?
What will God say to us as he considers our stewardship of
his resources?

But then there is the other question: *What if we do?*

What if we become intentional about leveraging our
resources for the Kingdom? What could we be a part of?

It's an amazing thought.

Generous givers want to do their part to get the gospel
to the ends of the earth. They want to be the generation that
sees the Great Commission fulfilled. They know that they
can shape eternity.

OUR GENEROSITY AFFECTS ETERNITY

In Luke's account of the woman who anointed Jesus' feet with expensive perfume, Jesus says to the host, Simon the Pharisee:

> "I tell you, her sins—and they are many—have been forgiven, so she has shown me much love. But a person who is forgiven little shows only little love."
> LUKE 7:47

While Jesus' words are still echoing, Luke—not coincidentally—tells us about three other women:

> Soon afterward Jesus began a tour of the nearby towns and villages, preaching and announcing the Good News about the Kingdom of God. He took his twelve disciples with him, along with some women who had been cured of evil spirits and diseases. Among them were Mary Magdalene, from whom he had cast out seven demons; Joanna, the wife of Chuza, Herod's business manager; Susanna; and many others who were contributing from their own resources to support Jesus and his disciples.
> LUKE 8:1-3

So, who were these women? We have Mary Magdalene, whom the Bible tells us had been demon-possessed. Joanna was the wife of Chuza, a man who managed Herod's household. Because of her husband's role, Joanna was probably wealthy. And finally, we have Susanna, who is mentioned as an example of "many others" who were generously "contributing from their own resources to support Jesus and his disciples."

Like the woman in Luke 7, God did something in all three of these women's lives, and they decided to leave their old life, follow Jesus, and live generously.

Here's what we can learn from these women:

Lesson #1: The more we grasp the reality of our forgiveness, the more our love for God and others will grow.

As we grow in our walk with Jesus, our view of his righteousness should increase, and our view of our own righteousness should diminish. The growing gap between those two is *grace*. So our understanding of the grace we have been given through forgiveness should grow over time.

Grace not only compels us to love God, but to love others as well. "We love each other because he loved us first" (1 John 4:19).

As we love God more, we should begin to see what he sees and love what he loves.

And that is *everyone*.

19

As we learn to view the world from God's perspective, we will begin to see that he put us where we are for a purpose. To make a difference. So we put others before ourselves. And when we put others first, generosity is the natural result.

We give because God has given to us. We give in response to his generosity.

Mary Magdalene, Joanna, and Susanna put others before themselves, "contributing from their own resources to support Jesus and his disciples" (Luke 8:3).

They understood what God had given them, and they responded by giving generously.

Lesson #2: When we are generous, we shape eternity.

I often hear people say, "I want to make a difference."

My response: "Great! God has designed you for this, and giving is a tangible part of making a difference."

Randy Alcorn wrote my favorite generosity quote: "Giving is a giant lever positioned on the fulcrum of this world, allowing us to move mountains in the next world. Because we give, eternity will be different—for others and for us."[6]

What about Mary Magdalene, Joanna, and Susanna? How did God use the resources they gave to shape eternity?

Let's catch up with them in Luke 24:1-10.

On the morning of Jesus' resurrection, some women

bringing spices to properly prepare his body found an empty tomb instead. An angel appeared to these women, reminding them of Jesus' words. The women then ran back to tell the disciples.

Who were these women?

Luke tells us.

> They rushed back from the tomb to tell his eleven disciples—and everyone else—what had happened. It was Mary Magdalene, Joanna, Mary the mother of James, and several other women who told the apostles what had happened.
> LUKE 24:9-10

Mary Magdalene and Joanna are named as those who first saw the empty tomb. Perhaps Susanna was included among the "several other women."

How's that for impact? How's that for an eternal return on investment? At that joyous moment, they certainly were not regretting having financially supported Jesus.

God wants you to live generously and be part of advancing his Kingdom by making Jesus known in your community and beyond.

Are you ready to follow in the footsteps of these women, using your resources to shape eternity? Are you ready to store up treasures in heaven?

LIVE FOR SOMETHING MORE

Preservation depends on destination.

I went to the funeral of a man who had poured out his life and possessions for the sake of others and the gospel. I also went to the funeral of a man who spent his entire life accumulating money and possessions. One man is experiencing an eternity with significant treasure. The other is experiencing an eternity with significantly less.

You may be familiar with these words from Jesus:

> Don't store up treasures here on earth, where moths eat them and rust destroys them, and where thieves break in and steal. Store your treasures in heaven, where moths and rust cannot destroy, and thieves do not break in and steal.
>
> MATTHEW 6:19-20

Those who spend their lives accumulating and hoarding resources for themselves will see everything taken away from them—in an instant. When their breath ceases, so does any hope their resources provide. Their houses, their cars, and the money in their bank accounts will no longer be useful to them.

Those who want to see their resources preserved must leverage them for God's eternal Kingdom. When we give, and give generously, our earthly treasures are transformed into eternal treasures. That's how we store up treasures in heaven.

When we leverage resources for the Kingdom, we shape eternity. God has rigged the system so that our generosity contributes to changing lives for all eternity.

When we give, we help to restore broken marriages.

When we give, we help to feed the hungry.

When we give, we help prodigals return home.

When we give, we help community members put their faith in Jesus.

When we give, we help start new churches.

When we give, we help send missionaries around the world.

When we give, we help get the gospel to unreached people groups.

When we give, we help fulfill the Great Commission.

When we give, we shape eternity for ourselves and others.

Live for something more.

Give generously.

Shape eternity.

WHERE DO YOU GO FROM HERE?

1. Read Luke 8:1-3. What stands out to you in the text?

2. Write your own salvation story. What did God do in your life?

3. God invites us into his mission. What are three ways you would like to see God use the resources you give?

4. Pray for God to leverage the resources you give to change lives in your neighborhood, community, and world. And thank him for allowing you to participate in his mission.

3

ACKNOWLEDGING THAT
GOD OWNS EVERYTHING

Though originally created in 1860, the modern version of The Game of Life was first published by Milton Bradley in 1960. You may know the famous board game simply as Life.

Life was a game I always enjoyed as a child. Our version had an insertable hill and buildings that added a 3D element to the board. Sadly, my kids play with an updated version that contains different rules and no insertable buildings. They don't know what they're missing. My version was better than their version. Going over that 3D hill was something special.

But whether you play with the better, older version or the lesser, updated version, the course of the game is the same: The box is opened, the pieces are laid out, the players spin the wheel, and then they drive their little plastic cars around the board, accumulating as much stuff as they can during their "lifetime." When the game is over, all the pieces go back in the box. Everything we thought we had is no longer ours.

Maybe the game reflects life more accurately than we'd care to admit. For, at the end of our days, all the stuff we've accumulated, whether much or little, is left behind for those who are still playing the game.

We can't take it with us.

Why? Because it's not our stuff. You can't keep what you don't own.

Mine might be the silliest word in the English language.

As a parent, I hear my kids use this word a lot. That basketball is *mine*. That stuffed animal is *mine*. That football card is *mine*. That toy is *mine*. That snack is *mine*. That toothbrush is *mine*. (Yes, my family has toothbrush issues. Please don't judge us.)

Mine is a word that we've tried to eliminate at our house. As you can tell, we haven't been entirely successful. Still, we regularly remind our kids that everything in our possession is not actually our stuff. It belongs to God. God owns everything.

Truly understanding and believing this principle has dramatically altered the way eternity-shaping givers view possessions.

GOD OWNS EVERYTHING

In Matthew 25:14-30, Jesus tells the parable of the servants, also known as the parable of the talents. In this story, we hear about a master who goes on a long journey. Prior to leaving, he entrusts three servants with some financial resources to manage on his behalf while he's away. One receives five bags of silver, one receives two bags of silver, and the third receives one bag of silver. They are to do what the master would do with the resources if he were there.

Upon the master's return, he calls the servants to report on their management of the silver. Two of the servants have doubled their holding of silver, and the master praises them accordingly. However, the third servant, the one with the single bag of silver, simply tried to prevent loss by stashing the silver in a safe place. He didn't put the money to work in any way—not even depositing it in the bank, where it would have accrued interest. The third servant simply returned what he had been given, no more, no less. But the master isn't pleased. He condemns the third servant for his inaction.

Let me ask you a question: In the parable of the servants, who owns the silver?

When the master entrusted the bags of silver to his servants, did the transfer affect the ownership?

You know the answer.

The bags of silver always belonged to the master—before

his departure, during his time away, and when he returned. The silver was always his—and that includes the increase.

My first real paycheck came from a mini-golf and go-kart park. It was the perfect summer job for an eager fifteen-year-old. Since I wasn't deemed worthy to run the cash register, I was sent outside to manage the go-kart track.

My responsibility was simple: get people in and out of the go-karts without incident.

I spent hours upon hours with those go-karts. I knew which ones were fastest. I knew which one was terribly slow. I knew which ones had a slight steering problem. I knew which one was most likely to have its engine die during a race. I knew everything about those go-karts.

I was pretty much an expert in go-karts by the end of the summer, but at any point did those go-karts become *mine*?

The answer is no. My boss owned everything at the mini-golf place, including the go-karts. He simply *entrusted* me with those go-karts, to do what he would do if he were out there himself.

The very first verse of the Bible says, "In the beginning God created the heavens and the earth" (Genesis 1:1). Everything we see (and don't see) came into existence at his word. And because God created everything, he is the rightful owner of everything.

Now, is there any point in Scripture where we find God relinquishing his ownership of everything?

Again, you know the answer.

Like the master in the parable, God continues to own it all, regardless of who possesses what. He has simply *entrusted* us with a certain portion of what he owns. Between now and when Christ returns, or we pass from the face of the earth, our responsibility is to use God's resources the way that he would if he were here.

Just to be clear, anything we have in our hands, in the bank, or in our homes has been entrusted to us by God. Just because our name is on the title doesn't mean we're the owner. We are stewards, servants who have been entrusted by the ultimate owner to manage a portion of his assets.

Recognizing God's rightful ownership of *everything*, and our position as entrusted *servants*, releases our hearts from the material and monetary *possessiveness* that otherwise threatens to enslave and entrap us.

So, if we acknowledge that God is the owner, one question naturally follows: *What does he want us to do with all his stuff?*

THE ADVENTURE OF GENEROSITY

Back to the parable of the servants.

Before the master leaves on his journey, he hands his servants a total of eight bags of silver. When he returns, the servants hand him back fifteen bags of silver.

Stewardship is a word we often use to describe the management of God's resources. But we misunderstand God's intentions if we think that stewardship or management means "maintaining the status quo." What we find in the parable is *anything but* maintaining the status quo. The status quo is thoroughly condemned.

God does not entrust us with his resources so we can live insulated lives and not rock the boat.

When the master returned, something significant had happened, something that helps us understand what we should do with the resources in our possession. The master found his possessions had increased. Eight bags of silver had become fifteen bags of silver.

His ownership and his kingdom had grown. And those who helped expand his kingdom were celebrated.

That is the goal of stewardship—to grow God's Kingdom by introducing others to the love of Jesus. With everything we have been given, we are to grow God's Kingdom.

The responsibility is challenging. Accomplishing the goal requires risk. The celebrated servants certainly took risks. One does not double one's assets without risk. But please understand: Taking appropriate risks does not mean being foolish or impulsive. Rather, the faithful servants made wise use of the resources entrusted to them, relying on God for the ultimate growth to gain a full return.

Such is the Christian life—a life in which risk and

certainty find themselves intertwined. We risk our resources and our lives for the advancement of God's Kingdom while trusting in the certainty of our Master's victory.

God has entrusted you with possessions so more will know of his love. Your bank account. Your house. Your car. Your education. All of it is to be leveraged for God's Kingdom. Our prayer should not be "Do you want me to leverage this resource?" but "*How* do you want me to leverage this resource?"

The resources are all *his* anyway.

When we understand that God owns everything and that he has entrusted us with certain resources for our time on earth—and that our time here is but a moment in eternity—we are not concerned about whether God has given us a little or a lot, because we are focused on leveraging whatever we have been given.

Our mission is clear. We are to use whatever possessions God has entrusted to us for the advancement of his Kingdom. God wants to see more people put their faith in Jesus, and he has created us and commissioned us to be part of the mission.

Stewardship is not about maintaining the status quo; it is an endeavor that requires risk and offers reward. Stewardship is an adventure-filled journey, with unexpected twists and turns. But through it all, we trust in God and his promises. The generous life is a life of risk and certainty.

Generous givers know that everything in their possession is owned by God. And everything in your possession is owned by God as well.

WHERE DO YOU GO FROM HERE?

1. Read Matthew 25:14-30. What are three things that stand out to you?

2. Think of someone you've known, or heard of, who passed away, leaving behind significant assets. How does his or her death affect your view of your possessions?

3. What are some creative (and possibly risky) ways you could leverage the resources God has given you to advance his Kingdom?

4. Pray that God will help you realize that he is the rightful owner of all your possessions. Ask him to show you ways to leverage the resources he has entrusted to you for his Kingdom.

4

FUELED BY GRATITUDE

What if I told you that there is something you could try that has been proven to increase heart health, enhance physical well-being, increase the likelihood that you will engage in heathier activities, and help you sleep longer and better?

What if I told you that this same thing has been linked to increased life satisfaction, happiness, subjective well-being, and optimism?

And it helps prevent burnout at work.

And it helps you become a better employee.

And it helps decrease materialism.

And it increases the likelihood you'll perceive stressful situations as opportunities for growth.

And it strengthens relationships—especially marriage and family relationships.

I can hear you now: "Sign me up. Tell me your secret."

I have good news for you. There's no sign-up needed, no elixir to swallow, and no secret to discover.

It is available for anybody and everybody.

It's called *gratitude*.

The benefits of gratitude are widely documented. Like the relationship between generosity and happiness, researchers have extensively studied the benefits of a thankful heart.

Simply stated: Gratitude is good for you.

THE GENESIS OF GRATITUDE

When I was a pastor, I always enjoyed seeing Jerry—even in church business meetings. Jerry was a longtime member of the church. He was humble, kind, and generous. Whenever the topic of generosity came up, he would say something like, "I don't see how I can't give. I am just so thankful for what God has done for me."

Where does gratitude come from? The answer is largely tied to an absence of entitlement.

To put it bluntly, it's hard to feel gratitude for things you think you deserve or have earned.

Feeling entitled is almost certain to ensure a lack of gratitude. Believing that we deserve something good can easily lead to disappointment when our expectations aren't met. Rarely does it lead to gratitude.

Imagine a seesaw, with gratitude on one side and entitlement on the other. As one goes up, the other goes down. When you consider what we *actually* deserve, as sinful creatures, and what we have received by God's grace and Christ's sacrifice, Christians should be the most grateful and gracious people on the planet. Our hearts should effuse thankfulness.

Romans 3:23 tells us that "everyone has sinned; we all fall short of God's glorious standard."

There's no exception clause in that verse. "Everyone" means *everyone*. One hundred percent of humanity. The condition that began in the Garden of Eden continues to this day. We're all sinners.

And sin comes with consequences.

If we want to talk about entitlement—what we deserve, what we've earned—we don't need to look any further than Romans 6:23: "The wages of sin is death."

We have earned death. We deserve death. Not a nice house. Not a full bank account. Not an exotic vacation. Not an incredible pair of shoes or an expensive car.

Death.

What that means is that anything we receive that isn't *death* is reason for gratitude. Every good thing—from your morning cup of coffee to your family, job, health, home—is an undeserved gift from God.

But wait, there's more. There is a tiny little conjunction—*but*—in Romans 6:23, and what follows that conjunction changes everything: "but the free gift of God is eternal life through Christ Jesus our Lord."

We are given a "free gift" through the work of Jesus. Because of his sacrifice, we are no longer condemned to death but have been gifted an eternal relationship with God.

In the span of a single verse, we went from death to eternal life. Not because of anything we did, but because Jesus did everything.

Once we realize that we are entitled to nothing, we are freed up to be grateful for everything. As Paul said to the Christians in Corinth, "What do you have that God hasn't given you?" (1 Corinthians 4:7).

When you consider that we have been given eternal life instead of the death we deserve, our gratitude should know no bounds.

GOD'S GOOD GIFTS

According to the book of James, God is the giver of all good things (James 1:17). God certainly gave us the ultimate gift when he gave us Jesus, but he didn't stop there. He continues to pour out gifts in abundance.

At times in life it can be difficult to recognize God's good gifts. Sometimes this is due to an external factor, such as the death of a loved one. Sometimes it's because of an internal factor, such as dissatisfaction with our standard of living. We can't see the good right in front of us because our sights are set on something else.

The next time your heart struggles to recognize God's gifts in your life, take a moment to consider three areas of God's generosity: relational, physical, and spiritual.

Relational generosity

God created us to live in relationship with other people. God brings people into our lives to help us, shape us, comfort us, and challenge us. They are friends, coworkers, family members, and church members. Some of us will have a lot of relationships, which extroverts love. Others will have only a few, close people in their lives, which is an introvert's dream. But whether few or many, every relationship is a good gift from God.

Physical generosity

A roof over our heads. Food on the table. Clothes on our backs. A car to drive.

We take for granted most of the physical gifts God has given us. Every day we are surrounded by blessings from God, blessings that many people around the world would love to have. Yet we consider them mundane, even take them for granted. We go through the day with all these benefits while rarely pausing to thank God for these good gifts.

Spiritual generosity

While God's relational and physical generosity toward us is significant, the greatest gift he's given us is Jesus. There was no one less deserving of death than Jesus, and no one more deserving than you and me. Christ's sacrifice brought us from life to death. His sacrifice provides us with real hope. His sacrifice changes everything about our present and future lives.

What can happen when we really grasp God's generosity? Consider the example of Zacchaeus in Luke 19:1-10.

WHEN WE GET IT

Zacchaeus was a well-known and widely despised tax collector in the city of Jericho. Before he met Jesus, his heart was consumed with a deep desire to accumulate wealth.

Did he long for financial security? Did greater wealth make him feel more successful? We don't know. But we do know he was willing to sacrifice everything, including his reputation and relationships, to acquire wealth.

Suddenly, everything changed. Zacchaeus came to see his finances in a much different light. The money in his bank account represented not only regretful, sinful choices but also an opportunity to bless others in unexpected ways.

Why the dramatic shift? What happened to his heart?

It's simple; he met Jesus. Jesus offered to enter Zacchaeus's house and break bread with him. Jesus offered a relationship to Zacchaeus.

And Zacchaeus accepted.

Suddenly, Zacchaeus saw the world with new eyes. He saw that God had placed people around him, not for him to plunder but to provide for. Zacchaeus met Jesus, and it changed everything.

Zacchaeus recognized the gift he had been given, and his response was to give generously in return. I hope this is true for you as well.

Is there any more appropriate response to God's radical generosity toward us than to be generous toward others?

When we truly realize the gift we have been given, our eyes should be opened to a whole new reality. Our hearts should beat with renewed vigor.

Like Zacchaeus, we were once bound by our sinful desires to chase the things of this world. It was a fruitless existence that never brought satisfaction.

But then we met Jesus. That relationship rearranges everything in our hearts and provides a fulfilling purpose for our lives.

Do you see with the eyes of Zacchaeus? Do you see with the eyes of someone who has been given the greatest possible gift?

Are you grateful? If you are grateful, generosity will be

the natural outcome. Let the overflow of God's generosity toward you spill out as generosity toward others.

WHERE DO YOU GO FROM HERE?

1. Read the story of Zacchaeus in Luke 19:1-10. What stands out to you in the story?

2. Consider the relational, physical, and spiritual gifts you have been given and name five things for which you are thankful. Now take a moment to thank God for all his blessings in your life.

3. How would you describe a consistently grateful person? What characteristics would such a person have? Likewise, how would you describe a consistently ungrateful person?

4. What can you do today to allow your gratitude to spill over into generosity toward others?

5

GIVING AS AN ACT OF TRUST

I was standing on a small wooden ledge, high up in a tree, and they wanted me to jump.

How did I find myself in this situation?

My wife and I had decided to go on a double date with a couple in our neighborhood. Most couples would probably go out to dinner and a movie, but we decided to do something different.

Not far from our house, there is a high ropes course consisting of several obstacles set high off the ground amidst large trees. The challenge is to move from one obstacle to the next to complete the course. Though each person is attached by harness to a cable, the height of many of these obstacles can be unnerving.

On this particular obstacle, we were required to jump from a significant height and swing down into a vertically hung net, which would stop our momentum. Beneath and between the ledge and the net was only hard dirt and pine needles. If something went wrong—such as a rope or harness breaking—death or serious injury was a real possibility.

Up to this point in the ropes course, I had been fine, in large part because I had some sense of control. If something went wrong, I could hold on until help came. But this obstacle didn't offer that comfort.

I had to trust the cable and harness and jump.

I had to trust that the safety equipment would do exactly what it was supposed to do. I had to trust that the rope would allow me to swing into the net below.

I would be lying if I said that my knees weren't slightly weak at this point.

But with my ego and pride on the line (after all, my wife was watching), I jumped.

And it was incredible.

The rope and harness made good on their promise and allowed me to experience a rush I won't soon forget. When I hit the vertical net, my immediate thought was, *That was awesome! I want to do it again.*

A simple act of trust resulted in an adventure I could never have imagined before the jump.

Likewise, giving generously is an act of trust.

I remember meeting with a friend who was struggling financially. He and his wife had acquired a significant amount of debt over the years, and their current income barely covered the bills.

As I asked a series of questions, the topic of generosity came up. He admitted that their generosity was relatively insignificant. So I challenged him.

"Do you trust God?"

"I do."

"Do you believe the Bible tells us to give?"

"I do."

"So, do you trust God?"

He understood. Giving is an act of trust.

IN GOD WE TRUST

Have you ever found yourself thinking if you just had a little more in your savings account, then you would feel secure? Or if you had a certain amount in your retirement account, then all of your concerns would vanish?

You're not alone.

Though the American dollar reads, "In God We Trust," many Americans have greater faith in the green paper it's printed on.

Most people would rather feel they are in control of their

situation. We'd all like to believe we can handle whatever life throws our way.

This significantly affects the way we handle our finances. We often view money as the solution to our problems and our protection against the unforeseen. We lean on money for comfort, security, peace, and sustenance.

And because we've placed our hope in our financial security, like the rich young ruler we're reluctant to part with any of our resources.

In chapter 1, we considered 1 Timothy 6:17-19, where Paul tells Timothy to communicate a message to those who are considered rich in his church.

As you reread verses 17 and 18, focus on what Paul says about trust:

> Teach those who are rich in this world not to be proud and not to trust in their money, which is so unreliable. Their trust should be in God, who richly gives us all we need for our enjoyment. Tell them to use their money to do good. They should be rich in good works and generous to those in need, always being ready to share with others.
> 1 TIMOTHY 6:17-18

Money is untrustworthy and unreliable. If you put your trust in money, you will find your feelings of security fluctuating with the stock market. When the market's up, you feel good. When the market drops, so do your spirits. That's a terrible way to live.

I have met many people who seem to think that a certain level of income or money in the bank will eliminate all their concerns. But when they get that increased paycheck or achieve their savings goal, their concerns do not subside. They may even get bigger, because now there's more to lose. So they continue their pursuit of an even bigger paycheck or even more money in the bank. It is a brutal, disappointing, and never-ending cycle.

The goalposts shift. Enough is never enough. The human heart never has its fill.

Giving is not about providing for God's needs. He already owns everything. He's not waiting for your financial gifts so he can finally move forward with his plans. He can and will move forward regardless of your generosity.

Giving is ultimately for *your* benefit. It is an act of trust. It is a visible demonstration of your reliance on God's provision and promises. God uses giving to mold your heart into a heart that trusts him more.

Giving says to God, "I trust you more than I trust myself or money."

Giving causes you to lean into God. Hoarding pulls you away from him. Giving demonstrates your reliance on God. Hoarding demonstrates self-reliance.

GOD'S PROMISES

Throughout the Bible, when God tells us to trust him with our financial resources, there is often a promise tied to our act of trust.

What promises and provisions are we trusting when we give generously to God? We're trusting that he will provide, that he will multiply, that he will enrich.

God promises he will provide

Malachi 3:10 is one of the better-known verses on generosity.

> "Bring all the tithes into the storehouse so there will be enough food in my Temple. If you do," says the LORD of Heaven's Armies, "I will open the windows of heaven for you. I will pour out a blessing so great you won't have enough room to take it in! Try it! Put me to the test!"

Typically, this verse is used to demonstrate the importance of proportional giving—that is, giving according to what God has given us. And while proportional giving is important, we sometimes miss the second half of the verse, which includes a significant promise.

God doesn't tell us to give and then just leave us hanging. No, he ties a promise to our generosity. He promises to pour out an abundance of blessings on us. And he tells us to *test* him in this, to give him the opportunity to show that he will make good on his promise.

Let me repeat that: God tells us to *test* his promise. That's incredible.

Does this mean that giving generously to the church will finally get you that red Lamborghini you've dreamed of? Does it mean you'll have more than enough in your retirement account? Does it even mean you will get the pay increase you desire?

Not necessarily. We don't see the widow with the two coins at the Temple treasury in Luke 21:1-3 suddenly become a gazillionaire. We don't see the poor but generous Macedonians in 2 Corinthians 8:1-4 driving brand-new, gold-plated chariots.

God's blessings can be financial and material. But they can also be spiritual. Maybe God gives you the contentment you have been chasing for years, the same contentment you once sought from money. Maybe God shows you how to become part of something far more significant than your own momentary life on earth.

Can God provide material needs? Of course. And he often does. As Jesus said,

Look at the birds. They don't plant or harvest or store food in barns, for your heavenly Father feeds them. And aren't you far more valuable to him than they are?

MATTHEW 6:26

God often provides something that resonates more deeply within our souls. This book is ultimately not about money or generosity. It's about your heart. God wants your heart to reflect his heart. And your heart wants to reflect God's heart. God uses financial generosity to satisfy that longing.

"Test me," God says. "I will provide. I will bless."

But it takes trust.

God promises he will multiply

In John 6:1-15, Jesus and his disciples are watching a crowd that has been following Jesus. Jesus asks Philip, one of his disciples, where they can buy bread to feed everyone, for the crowd had not eaten in a while. Philip points out the obvious impossibility of providing everyone with bread. The closest they come is finding a boy with five loaves and two fish.

Can you relate to that boy? You look at your meager resources and wonder what God could ever do with them in the face of such a great need. What difference can your generosity make?

A big difference, it turns out, because our God is a multiplying God.

When the boy generously gives up his food, Jesus takes the meal, blesses it, and begins to break it into pieces.

And the breaking doesn't stop. Jesus keeps multiplying the bread and fish until everyone in the crowd has eaten their fill. Even then, there are twelve baskets full of leftovers.

Or what about the widow and Elijah in 1 Kings 17:8-16?

A drought has struck the land, and Elijah finds himself by a dried-up brook. God tells Elijah to travel to Zarephath, near Sidon, where he will meet a widow who will provide him with food. Elijah does as he's told and locates the widow whom God has mentioned. When Elijah asks for some water and bread, the widow reveals her dire situation.

> I swear by the LORD your God that I don't have a
> single piece of bread in the house. And I have only a
> handful of flour left in the jar and a little cooking oil
> in the bottom of the jug. I was just gathering a few
> sticks to cook this last meal, and then my son and I
> will die.
> 1 KINGS 17:12

Elijah encourages her not to fear but to trust in God's provision—to first prepare food for Elijah and then for herself and her son. That was an uncomfortable request. He was asking her to sacrifice her final meal. Yet the widow does as Elijah requested. She provides him with water and bread before making bread for herself and her son.

And God multiplies her faithful offering.

Though the widow assumes this will be the last meal she and her son will consume, God has a different outcome in mind. The jar of flour and the jug of oil do not run empty. God continues to fill both containers with the necessary means to bake more bread—not just for that meal but for the duration of the drought.

God promises multiplication when we trust him. Second Corinthians 9:10 says, "God is the one who provides seed for the farmer and then bread to eat. In the same way, he will provide and increase your resources and then produce a great harvest of generosity in you."

God will take whatever you give and multiply your resources to accomplish his purposes. That is a promise from God.

But it takes trust.

God promises he will enrich

You probably enjoy getting a good return on your investments (ROI). You put your money where you hope its value will increase, and you pull your money from investments that decrease in value.

You like a good ROI. I like a good ROI. And so does God.

Therefore, God promises to enrich those who give. In 2 Corinthians 9:11, Paul writes to those who trust God with their money: "Yes, you will be enriched in every way so that you can always be generous."

We find a similar promise in Proverbs 11:25: "The generous will prosper; those who refresh others will themselves be refreshed."

And we see this promise again in the parable of the servants, when the master takes the silver from the servant who did nothing with it and gives it to the servant who most greatly multiplied his resources.

God wants a good ROI. Therefore, he enriches those who trust him and give generously.

God does not enrich the generous so that they can have big houses, luxury cars, and more lavish vacations. He enriches them so that they "can always be generous" (2 Corinthians 9:11).

God gives so that we can give. He blesses so that we can bless others.

God is looking for conduits of generosity, channels through which his blessings can flow. He is looking for men and women whom he can enrich so that others may be blessed.

Do you want God to enrich you? I cannot tell you *how* he will do it, but here's what I know—he has promised to do it.

But it takes trust.

GENEROSITY IS AN ACT OF TRUST

Generosity shifts our hearts from reliance on ourselves and money to reliance on God. Generous giving visibly demonstrates our trust in God and his promises to provide.

If you are a Christian, you have already trusted God with your soul. It's time that you trust him with your money.

Are you ready to take the leap? Are you ready to experience what God wants for you, the thrill that accompanies openhanded living? It is time to get off the ledge and take the plunge.

WHERE DO YOU GO FROM HERE?

1. Read God's promises in Malachi 3:10 and 2 Corinthians 9:6-11. How do these verses affect your view of generosity?

2. How is trust in God connected to your generosity?

3. Consider some financial areas of your life where you find it difficult to trust God. What would it look like for you to fully trust God with your finances?

4. Spend some time praying that God will help you trust him and his promises.

6

GENEROSITY AS
AN ACT OF WORSHIP

One Sunday, when our boys were young, we had two of them in the worship service with us. At their ages, this was always a risk. Usually they were in the children's ministry area during the service, but this morning they wanted to join us. It felt like we were sitting next to a couple of ticking time bombs. We never knew what they would do or say—or when.

If you're a parent, you can probably relate.

Prior to leaving the house that morning, our boys had asked if they could give their offering money in the grown-up service. As they frantically jumped up and down, they raised their ziplock bags filled with quarters, dimes, nickels, and pennies.

As a guy who regularly talks and teaches about money

and generosity, I felt proud. I sensed I had accomplished something significant as a parent.

My kids were worshipful givers.

I had taught them well.

If only more parents could be like me.

That's what I was thinking.

Back then, our church used large, plastic buckets to collect the offering. When the bucket was handed to me, I passed it along to my son who was sitting next to me.

Lifting his bag full of coins, he opened the top and dumped the contents into the bucket.

The coins hit the bottom of the bucket with a resounding *crashhhhhh!*

There was no mistaking what had just happened, and everyone turned toward us, chuckling.

Then my son passed the bucket down the row.

I'm not sure what he thought was going to happen when he gave, but as he watched the bucket continue down the row, it began to dawn on him that his money was gone. The further the bucket went, the more his anxiety grew.

"Wait!" he yelled. "How do I get my money back?"

And just like that, my proud dad moment was undone by the laughter of the congregation.

My son clearly did not understand the connection between giving and worship. He was *not* a generous giver after all.

But he's not the only one.

For many people, the offering is simply part of the church service, a necessity to endure. They understand that it allows the church to pay the pastor, the staff, and the utility bills, and they give (or don't give) accordingly.

But for eternity-shaping givers, the offering is much more than just a necessary part of the service. It is an act of worship.

WHAT IS WORSHIP?

"The offering time is so boring. I wish we could just skip it and get back to worshiping." Comments like these are common in many churches. Maybe you've had similar thoughts yourself.

Before moving forward, we must tackle an important question: *What exactly is worship?*

If you were to ask most people in the church this question, they would likely say something about singing or music. And that's an understandable response. When the church's music leader says, "Please stand and worship with me," the congregation stands up and sings. When people talk about church, they typically separate the service into three categories: the worship time (singing), the offering and announcements, and the sermon.

But is *worship* just a Christian code word for *music*?

No. Music in a church service is usually considered *part* of worship, but worship is much broader than that. In simple terms, *worship* means to ascribe worth to something. Another way to say it is "show reverence." As Christians, we ascribe worth to God, showing reverence for his power, authority, character, and holiness. And though one way to do this is by singing songs of praise and adoration in our church services, we show our reverence for God in other ways as well. The apostle Paul tells us that we are to worship God with our entire lives:

> Dear brothers and sisters, I plead with you to give your bodies to God because of all he has done for you. Let them be a living and holy sacrifice—the kind he will find acceptable. This is truly the way to worship him.
> ROMANS 12:1

Worshiping God with our whole lives includes our giving. Unfortunately, many believers act as if the offertory is like the intermission at a play, a time to take a quick break between the more important elements of the church service.

But our giving is so much more than that. It is one way that we demonstrate our reverence for God, just as we do through our singing. Giving can and should be a heartfelt act of worship—whether during or apart from a church service.

THE WOMAN WHO WORSHIPED THROUGH GIVING

In Luke 7:36-50, we find Jesus having dinner at Simon the Pharisee's house. During the meal, a woman enters who is identified only as "a certain immoral woman." In her hands is an alabaster jar of perfume, likely worth a year's wages or more. The woman kneels behind Jesus at his feet and begins to weep. As her tears begin to drip onto Jesus' feet, the woman takes down her hair to wipe them away.

Next, she opens the bottle of perfume and begins to anoint Jesus' feet. If by now the woman hasn't caught the attention of everyone in the room, the strong scent of the expensive perfume certainly will. All eyes are on Jesus and the woman.

Jesus then tells Simon a story about two people who were loaned an amount of money—five hundred pieces of silver to one and fifty pieces to the other—and neither one could repay the debt. But then the lender cancels both debts, and Jesus asks, "Who do you suppose loved him more after that?"

"I suppose the one for whom he canceled the larger debt," Simon replies.

Jesus agrees and then points out that the woman at his feet has shown great love because she has been shown great forgiveness. She had recognized the generosity that Jesus had bestowed on her, and she had responded by generously using one of her most valuable possessions to honor Jesus.

She worshiped Jesus through her deep, heartfelt generosity.

A friend of mine told me about Gene and Marcy, an elderly couple at a church in Georgia. They had been members of the church for many years. They loved the church and they loved Jesus.

Gene and Marcy requested a meeting with their pastor, which was unusual for the couple. After talking with the pastor, they pulled out a checkbook and wrote a check for $100,000.

Gene and Marcy told the pastor that God had given them much in their lives. They decided to put their money toward something that would demonstrate the worth they ascribed to their generous God. So they gave generously to support the mission of the church.

Gene and Marcy worshiped through giving.

HOW TO CULTIVATE A HEART THAT WORSHIPS THROUGH GIVING

"I am not sure if I can honestly say I worship through giving," a church member once said to me. "I give, but I don't know if it's an act of worship for me. It feels detached."

For many, giving feels obligatory and routine.

What can we do about this?

We can cultivate hearts that worship through giving by focusing on gratitude, prayer, and praise. Here are a few suggestions to get you started.

Consider what God has done for you

Worshipful givers are fueled by gratitude. Consider the good gifts God has given you. Start with the essentials (food, clothing, shelter, etc.) and continue from there. Most important, focus on your ability to have a relationship with God through the sacrifice of Jesus. There is no greater gift.

Prayerfully seek God about your generosity

Involve God in your giving decisions. Many people who feel detached from their giving are not communicating with God about their generosity. Too often, our financial fears and insecurity limit the amount we give. Ask God what *he* would like you to give. Ask him to open your eyes to the needs that you can meet. Seek his guidance before you give.

Ask God to multiply your gifts in unimaginable ways

God can multiply the gifts you give in unbelievable ways. He can take the resources you provide to feed the hungry, heal broken marriages, and get the gospel to the ends of the earth. Pray that he will use your resources and the resources of others for these purposes.

Praise God for how he uses your generosity

What is God doing in and through your church? Did someone accept Jesus as their Lord and Savior? Are the homeless being cared for? Are church-supported missionaries sharing the gospel on the other side of the world? Praise God for allowing you to participate in his mission on earth.

During the offertory time at church, or prior to your online giving, thank God for his generosity, ask him to multiply the impact of your gifts, and praise him for the Kingdom-advancing work that has already been accomplished.

IS IT OKAY TO GIVE ONLINE?

The short answer is yes. It is okay to give online. Many churches opened this avenue for giving during the Covid-19 lockdown, and many church members have found that it simplifies the process of giving. Online giving doesn't have to diminish your sense of worship. What matters is your heart and how it is attuned to worshiping and honoring God with your giving.

Like many others, I give to my church online—for several reasons. It is convenient, safe, reduces my church's administrative costs, and eases church budgeting. Most important, it ensures that I always put God first in my finances.

Online giving helps me align with God's design for my

money—to be a conduit through which his generosity flows. For me, setting up automatic giving is an act of commitment and discipline.

But not everyone has the same experience with online giving. In fact, there are some people who probably should not do their giving online.

Here are three signs that online giving may not be right for you:

1. *You no longer think about your giving.* Even though you're still giving, the automatic withdrawal has eliminated any worshipful thought about it. The money is deducted from your checking account, and you rarely stop to consider it. Your giving has become more like a payroll tax deduction from your paycheck. You may stop for a moment to think when you receive your end-of-the-year contribution statement, but otherwise the spiritual act of worship through giving is pretty much dead.

2. *Your giving feels obligatory and disconnected from the church's mission.* Giving to your local church should make you feel more connected, not less. But if the click of a button on an app or a website makes you feel isolated from your contribution, you may not want to do your giving online.

3. *You feel that online giving hurts your ability to lead by example.* I hear this most often from pastors. By not giving during the church service, they feel they are missing an opportunity to lead by example. Parents may feel this way as well. If this is a significant concern for you, online giving may not be right for you.

Online giving is a method that works for some but not for others. Whatever method you choose, be certain to maintain heartfelt, spiritual involvement.

GENEROSITY IS AN ACT OF WORSHIP

Generous giving is not meant to be a sterile or detached act. Like the woman in Luke 7, generously pouring out her resources to ascribe worth to Jesus, we should demonstrate our heartfelt reverence for God through our giving.

The offertory is not a musical interlude during the church service. Rather, it is a time to consider what God has provided, what he has already accomplished, and what he might be calling you to invest in with your giving.

Is generosity more than just a transaction for you? Do you worship through your giving?

WHERE DO YOU GO FROM HERE?

1. Read Luke 7:36-50. How does the story about the woman with the alabaster jar influence your approach to giving?

2. How have you viewed the concept of worship in the past? How does generous giving fit into your understanding of worship?

3. Plan for your next offering. Decide in advance what you will do during the offertory time. Will you consider what God has done for you, ask God to multiply your gifts in unimaginable ways, or praise Him for how he uses your generosity?

4. Pray about your generosity. Ask God to guide your giving. Pray that he will multiply your gifts to advance his Kingdom and bring glory to his name.

7

GIVING CAN BE MESSY

My friends Justin, Kasey, and their six-month-old son needed a place to stay. They were moving from Texas to North Carolina in January, but their lease ended in October. A two-month extension on their lease was not an option.

What would they do?

Justin remembered a conversation with Dennis, a fellow church member, a few months back. Dennis had said that he and his wife, Michelle, would be happy to host Justin and his family if they ever needed a place to stay. They had two kids of their own, both in diapers.

So, was the offer still good? Were Dennis and Michelle still willing to take in another couple ... with a baby ... for two months ... over the holidays?

Indeed, they were. When Justin called to inquire, Dennis and Michelle welcomed his family into their home.

For the next two months, life in the house was anything but calm, clean, and sterile. It was messy. There was often a baby crying, biting, or feeling sick. When one child decided not to sleep at night, no one slept at night. Tired eyes were just part of the package.

There was a distinct odor that needed to be dealt with. Three children in diapers will do that. The couples designated an outdoor trash can as their diaper dumpster.

Two months later, Justin and Kasey completed their move to North Carolina.

Though life in Dennis and Michelle's house was sometimes chaotic and smelly, they look back on their hospitality with gratitude, not regret. They are grateful that God used them to help a family in need.

By the way, the two couples are now dear friends.

Generosity is not confined to the offering plate. Nor is it meant to be a sterile, detached act.

Biblical generosity is a well-lived-in home that is topsy-turvy from numerous guests.

Biblical generosity is giving to someone in need with no strings attached.

Biblical generosity is listening to a hurting friend, even if it ruins your day's plans.

True generosity is sometimes messy.

MESSY GENEROSITY

In the well-known parable of the Good Samaritan in Luke 10:30-37, a man walking down a road is attacked by robbers and left for dead without any valuables.

A priest traveling along the same road sees the beaten man but doesn't stop to help. Instead, he passes on the other side of the road. Later, a Levite also comes across the injured man on the roadside. But like the priest, he avoids the man and keeps on walking.

But there is another man—a Samaritan—traveling the same road. The Samaritans were a people group detested by the Jews. Certainly he will also pass by the man as well.

But he doesn't.

Instead, he goes to the bloodied man and bandages his wounds. Then the Samaritan puts the man on his donkey and takes him to an inn where he can heal and recover. The Samaritan tells the innkeeper to do whatever is necessary to care for the beaten man. He promises to cover whatever costs are involved.

When the Samaritan knelt by the bruised and naked man, he didn't just hand him a few coins and go on his way. Instead, he took some of his own oil, wine, and bandages and cared for the man physically.

The Samaritan's clothes, donkey, and other possessions were certainly soiled by the dirt and blood.

It was messy generosity.

On top of all that, the Samaritan did not place a financial limit on the man's care at the inn. It was open-ended and uncertain.

It was anything but sterile and tidy. It was messy generosity. God is looking for generous hearts that are willing to get messy.

GENEROSITY MEANS MORE THAN MONEY

Generously giving to our churches is certainly something we should all do. As the center of God's plan for reaching the world with the gospel, the church should be our first place of giving. But biblical generosity goes well beyond dropping a check into the offering plate or giving online. It isn't that neat and tidy.

God often calls us to get our hands dirty.

Like the Samaritan, a generous giver will be generous with more than money. Generosity isn't something we compartmentalize, giving freely to the church but hoarding everything else. True generosity goes viral, permeating every aspect of our lives. Money is only one of many areas that we are to hold with open hands. God calls us to be generous with our talents, time, and treasure as well.

Generosity looks like a dirty house

When we moved into our current home, my wife expressed her desire that our house would be leveraged for God's Kingdom. Sarah told me she hoped to see the house that God gave us become a gospel outpost in our neighborhood and community, a place where the love of Jesus would be evident. So we committed ourselves to being hospitable to whoever walked through the front door.

Or back door.

Or garage door.

You see, God has blessed us with three very active boys and has placed us in a neighborhood with numerous kids their age.

Those kids are also very active.

They track dirt and grass clippings into the house.

They smell sweaty and grimy from playing backyard football all day.

They eat a lot of food.

And we never know when they're going to show up.

But we enjoy opening our home to them and their parents in an effort to demonstrate the love of Jesus.

Do we have to run the vacuum more? Yes.

Do we occasionally find dents and marks on our walls? Yes.

Does the screen on our porch door get pushed in every other month? Yes.

But that's okay. We would rather have a well-loved gospel outpost than an immaculate and sterile, inwardly focused home.

Our house is messy on a regular basis. And that's a good thing.

Generosity looks like a "ruined" day (or night)

My wife was having some very concerning health issues. We decided she needed to go to the hospital. But we had a problem. It was evening, and we had three young boys at home.

What should we do?

I called up some good friends of ours, Chuck and Pam, and asked if they could help. They didn't hesitate. They agreed to watch our kids until we were able to return.

But the hospital visit wasn't quick. Hour after hour passed as we waited for the results of several tests. Evening turned to night and then to late night.

Sarah was released from the hospital around midnight. When we got home, we found our friends sleeping on our couches. Our boys were asleep in their beds.

Did they have other plans for that evening? They did. Did they have work the next morning? Absolutely.

I will never forget their generosity. They set aside their own needs to meet ours.

Opportunities to be generous with our time come in all shapes and sizes.

A friend needs someone to watch the kids so he can take his wife to the hospital.

A neighbor was just told by her husband that he wants a divorce. She is brokenhearted and needs someone to listen.

A coworker has a project due, but a family member just died. He needs someone to help complete the work so he can spend time with his family.

A church member is moving into a new apartment and needs some people to help load and unload the truck.

An acquaintance mentions feeling hopeless. It's obvious she needs to hear about Jesus.

Messy generosity will change your plans on a regular basis.

Generosity means giving without expecting a return

My friend Laura had a growing family. After their third child, it became apparent they needed a larger automobile to accommodate their family. Laura's husband is a pastor, and like many pastors, he doesn't make a lot of money. They don't complain. God called them to ministry for the mission, not the money.

But the need remained.

A family saw their need and decided to act. They provided Laura and her family with a van they never could have afforded on their own.

Laura and her husband will likely never be able to repay them.

In our world, giving often comes with expectations. The expectation of return may not surface immediately, but it can rear its ugly head at some point in the future.

"It would be nice if the Smiths watched our dog. We did it for them."

"Why wouldn't the Browns offer to cover the meal? We paid for them last time."

"I got her a gift. I can't believe she didn't get me one."

"They owe me."

But the generosity we find in the Bible is different. The Samaritan didn't expect his good deed to be repaid. He did it because it was the right thing to do. Biblical generosity is like that.

Biblical generosity is not *transactional*, where we give with an expectation of getting something in return. It is very one-sided. And it can be messy.

Generosity looks like being taken advantage of

Anthony told me one of his generosity stories. One day, he received a text from Michael, one of his old friends who lived several states away. Michael asked Anthony to pray for him and his family. He said he had been working multiple jobs to put food on the table but was still not generating enough income.

Anthony prayed for the family and decided to send them some money.

Later that week, he received another text from Michael, thanking him for the gift. At that moment, Anthony felt he had done the right thing.

Three weeks later, Michael posted a picture of himself on Facebook standing next to his brand-new Mercedes. Michael's wife commented on the post, telling Michael how good he looked with the new car.

Had Michael lied to Anthony? Had he exaggerated his need? Had he suddenly landed a high-paying new job? Or had Anthony made a bad financial decision in sending Michael some money?

Anthony didn't know. He never reached out to Michael to ask. He decided to let God deal with it. He had done what he thought was right at the moment, and he was content to leave it at that.

Now, don't misunderstand; we are not to be unwise givers. As managers of God's resources, we are to pursue wisdom in the ways we leverage his resources, including our generosity. But sometimes the risk we take on someone simply doesn't leave us with the hoped-for results. Sometimes we can feel taken advantage of.

I've been there. You probably have as well. Some will use these moments as an excuse not to give. But we cannot allow a few disappointments to stop us from living generously.

When these moments occur, we must recognize that generosity can be messy.

Generosity means helping people who hurt you

Jared's neighbor regularly had harsh words for him. He was always complaining about something. Jared's dogs barked too much. Jared's kids kicked their soccer ball onto his lawn again. Jared's yard needed better maintenance. This neighbor was tough to love, but Jared tried his best to remain calm and patient.

One day, Jared saw his neighbor on crutches, struggling to walk. The neighbor had been in a bad wreck, breaking his left leg and arm. In Jared's heart, he knew exactly what God wanted him to do.

Without being asked, Jared started mowing the neighbor's lawn while his kids pulled weeds from the flower bed.

When the neighbor opened his front door, Jared could tell that he wanted to say something harsh, but he didn't. Instead, he just said, "Thank you," and went back inside.

Those two words were the neighbor's first nonnegative comment to Jared. It was a step.

It's easy to bless and be generous with those who are close to us, those we are fond of, and those who are fond of us. But the generosity we see in Scripture places no such restrictions. In fact, we see something diametrically different. The sinner receives grace. The inflicter receives healing.

We all have people in our lives who bother us. There are people in our lives who have hurt us or abandoned us. We find it difficult to be around these people, and we can't fathom being generous to them. But Jesus makes the unfathomable a reality.

We are more like Jesus when we give to the undeserving than when we give to those we feel deserve it. In those moments of messy generosity, our hearts reflect the heart of God.

Generosity looks like involvement

Keith does something incredibly brave each Sunday: He volunteers in the middle school student ministry at our church. I have no clue how he endures, but week after week, he shows up to help middle schoolers learn more about their amazing God.

It is a picture of true courage.

Dana volunteers at an organization in Raleigh that provides gospel-centered social services to homeless, abused, and impoverished high-risk youth, individuals, and families.

I know that Keith and Dana give generously of their finances to their church, but their generosity doesn't stop with the click of a "Give Now" button on their computer screens. Their financial giving is not detached from the rest of their lives, because they recognize God's mission is not compartmentalized to just their finances.

Those who live with open hands will often find themselves doing much more than participating financially in God's mission. A heart that chases after God will find itself chasing the things God is after—the hearts of men and women.

Like the Good Samaritan, eternity-shaping givers don't sit on the sidelines. They help people who are hurting, care for the needy, counsel those who are broken, teach those who need to know more about God—and, yes, even serve in the middle school ministry.

Messy generosity means getting in the game and giving with no strings attached.

There is no better illustration of biblical generosity than the example of the one who was born in a dirty stable and later hung, bloody, beaten, and naked, on a rough wooden cross. He entered the mess we created so we could become clean. Follow his lead.

Expect the untidiness and complexity of biblical generosity. Allow your generosity to get messy.

WHERE DO YOU GO FROM HERE?

1. What stands out to you in the parable of the Good Samaritan (Luke 10:25-37)?

2. Why do you think some people avoid "messy" generosity? When considering the examples given in this chapter, which ones are most difficult for you?

3. What are some ways in which you can participate in messy generosity in your circle of influence?

4. Pray that God will provide you with an opportunity for messy generosity this week. And when he provides that opportunity, take it.

8

GIVING IS A PRIORITY

The year 2003 was a difficult one for my friend Scott and his wife. Due to circumstances beyond his control, Scott had to leave his pastoral role at a church.

Because Scott's job had provided for most of his family's needs, he immediately set out to find other sources of income. He found himself at a large retail chain, working anywhere between twelve and twenty-eight hours per week. Scott's wife picked up a job that offered her twenty-five hours per week.

Even with their substantially reduced incomes, Scott and his wife made giving the priority for their money. The decision was not easy. With bills to pay, and less coming in, their financial margin was razor thin. Nevertheless, they gave a portion of each paycheck to God, trusting him to meet their needs.

A little over a year later, Scott was hired by another church. When he and his wife looked at their bank account, they were shocked. They realized they had more money now than when Scott had left the first church.

It didn't make sense.

Scott could only provide one explanation: They had prioritized giving, and God had provided.

Scott has been at that church for seventeen years now. His story of faith and provision motivates him to help others experience what he and his wife experienced—a God who faithfully provides.

John 3:16 tells us that God gave his first and best, his one and only. God stepped out and demonstrated the firstfruits principle. He did not give us his leftovers. In sending Jesus, God showed us that giving our firstfruits is to be a priority.

Will you follow his lead?

Those who view money in light of eternity recognize that God gave us his first and best in Jesus, and therefore they make generosity a priority.

BIBLICAL GENEROSITY IS NOT ABOUT THE LEFTOVERS

For most people, generosity is something they think about only after the bills have been paid, the needs have been met, and some wants have been satisfied. Then they look at their bank account to see what's left. If there happens to be an amount they are comfortable giving away, they donate it.

The Bible teaches something radically different. Proverbs 3:9 says, "Honor the LORD with your wealth and with the best part of everything you produce." Some Bible translations say to give your "first produce of your entire harvest" (CSB). This teaching is known as the "firstfruits principle."

Throughout Scripture we are told to give our first and best to God. He's not looking for our financial leftovers. In 1 Corinthians 16:2, Paul tells the Corinthians to set something aside on the first day of the week. Setting aside an offering for God is the very first thing they are to do with their resources.

In Genesis 4, we read that two brothers, Cain and Abel, both presented offerings to God. Abel was a shepherd and presented the firstborn lambs from his flock to God. God was pleased with Abel's offering. Cain was a farmer and presented some of the land's produce to God. But unlike Abel's offering, God was not pleased with it.

Why was God pleased with Abel's offering but not Cain's? Does God prefer meat over vegetables?

Not really.

Hebrews 11:4 tells us that Abel's gift was offered in faith. He gave the firstborn, the best and most important of his flock. Abel didn't know whether there would be any more healthy births that season. It was possible that these firstborn lambs would be the only ones. But he trusted God more than he trusted his possessions. So, by faith, he gave the firstborn.

God's displeasure with Cain had nothing to do with whether God liked lima beans. God's displeasure was due to Cain's lack of faith. It is likely that the offering did not represent Cain's first and best. It likely represented what he could spare after his needs were already covered.

God didn't need an animal or a basket of vegetables. Both were already his. He wanted the heart of the giver to fully trust in him. Abel's gifts demonstrated the heart God desired, while Cain's gift did not.

Abel made giving a priority. Cain did not.

Biblical generosity is not about the leftovers.

PRIORITIZATION, PRACTICALLY

"But I'm not a shepherd or a farmer. The only animal I have is my dog, Fido, and I'm pretty sure God doesn't want me to sacrifice him."

Yes, the firstfruits principle was introduced in a society and time when most people were farmers and shepherds. So what does prioritized giving look like for us, practically?

For most of us, prioritizing our giving means we give a portion of our *gross income* before using the money for other purposes. This practice closely aligns with the firstfruits principle. Gross income is the amount we earn before taxes, insurance, and retirement are taken out.

Granted, the amount that hits our checking account is the net income (with taxes, insurance, and retirement taken out). Regardless, the amount we give is based on our gross income, and we give as soon as possible. When the paycheck hits our checking account, we give. Before the utilities are paid, before the debt payments are made, and before we start imagining what else we could do with the money, we give.

Prioritizing generosity is a big step. It completely reverses the way the rest of the world gives. They give out of their leftovers, while we give the choicest cuts before we ever take a bite.

Let's take the bull by the horns: Prioritizing generosity is a big step for people who are living on the financial edge or facing other financial challenges. What are we supposed to do when we aren't sure we can pay the bills and put food on the table? Should we stop giving until our financial challenges are resolved?

The question is understandable.

When facing financial difficulties and the temptation not to give arises, remember this: *God tells us to give*. He tells us to give not because he wants something from us, but because he wants something *for* us. We prioritize giving because it demonstrates our trust in God's promises and provision. And there is no better place in the world to place your trust.

God is the only one in this world who will deliver on all his promises.

Next, *the Bible does not provide an exclusion clause.* Nowhere in the Bible do we find a giving loophole or a verse about when we should not give. The Bible simply says that when God gives to us, we respond by giving.

Finally, *God delights in our obedience when obedience is difficult.* When we consider those in the Bible who are praised for their generosity, we find something surprising. Many were poor. The widow and her son in 1 Kings who were ready to starve? They were poor. The widow in Luke 21 who gave two coins? She was poor. The Macedonians mentioned in 2 Corinthians? They were poor.

Was generosity easy for any of them? Absolutely not. Their financial margin was nonexistent. If anyone had a reason not to give, it was them. But did they give? They did and were praised for it.

God delights in obedience when obedience is difficult.

WHERE DO YOU GO FROM HERE?

1. In light of Proverbs 3:9, why do you think many people give out of their leftovers?

2. What does John 3:16 reveal about prioritized generosity?

3. What are some ways you can make generosity a financial priority?

4. Thank God for leading you in the act of prioritized giving. Pray that he will give you the courage to follow his lead, even during difficult financial times.

9

GIVING PROPORTIONALLY

Ray, a college friend of mine, took a senior pastor role at a church in North Carolina. The church was mostly healthy except for one significant issue: Previous building projects had left the church more than a million dollars in debt, which was a large amount for their church. Many in the congregation didn't understand the impact this debt was having on their ability to do ministry, but Ray certainly did. The monthly debt payment was substantial.

More money could be going toward missions.

More money could help improve their children's ministry area.

More money could increase their ability to reach their community for Christ.

But "more money" wasn't there. It was all going toward their burdensome debt.

Ray and I had semiregular conversations about what could be done to reduce and eventually eliminate the debt. There was no easy solution unless someone wrote a million-dollar check. And that did not seem possible.

But one day, I received a text from Ray. The impossible had happened.

"Someone just gave us one million dollars to pay off the debt!"

"YES!!!" I replied.

Later, Ray told me that there was a man in his church who had made a significant amount of money through his business. Recognizing that God had given him an abundance, he felt responsible to give abundantly to advance God's Kingdom. Knowing the church's need, he decided to use the money to pay off the debt.

He gave proportionally.

Whether we have much or little, God calls us to give proportionally, according to what he has given us. The resources that God has entrusted to us are our guide for generosity. God's good gifts should be reflected in our giving.

GIVE ACCORDING TO WHAT YOU HAVE BEEN GIVEN

You may have heard of the word *tithe*, which simply means 10 percent. As previously mentioned, one of the most popular verses about tithing is Malachi 3:10:

"Bring all the tithes into the storehouse so there will be enough food in my Temple. If you do," says the LORD of Heaven's Armies, "I will open the windows of heaven for you. I will pour out a blessing so great you won't have enough room to take it in! Try it! Put me to the test!"

There are several other commands to tithe, or to give more than a tithe, in the Old Testament. God clearly establishes a pattern of proportional or percentage-based giving.

You won't find God telling us to give a specific dollar amount. Instead, he asks us to give according to what he has given us—that is, in proportion to what he has provided. In other words, there should be a direct correlation between the amount God provides and the amount we give.

A certain dollar amount per year may be the right amount for one person but not the next. The same amount may represent incredible generosity and faith for one person but a lack of generosity and faith for someone else.

Because of verses like Malachi 3:10, some will say that 10 percent is the right percentage. But rather than debate whether we should stick to a strict 10 percent, here is my suggestion: Make 10 percent your starting point. If you have yet to start giving, make 10 percent your goal. If you already give 10 percent, look for opportunities to give more. The Bible is filled with stories of people giving far beyond 10 percent of their resources.

The tithe was never meant to be an upper limit. Whatever amount you are giving of what God has entrusted to you, I encourage you to prayerfully consider increasing the proportion of your giving. Give according to what God has given you.

IS IT OKAY FOR ME TO REDUCE MY GIVING?

Jacob and his wife were consistently generous with their finances. As their income grew over the years, so did the amount they gave. They were a couple who truly gave by faith, putting God first in their finances.

But now they were facing a dilemma.

Jacob's company was not doing as much business as they once had. The downturn in revenue was likely going to mean a pay cut for Jacob. For the first time in a while, he and his wife were looking at their finances and wondering whether they could continue to give at the same level.

"Art, is it okay for me to reduce my giving?" he asked. "Or do I continue to give the same amount in faith?"

Jacob's question is a common one. People lose jobs. Incomes are reduced. What are we supposed to do when we face such a scenario?

Here's what I told Jacob:

1. *Giving is never about the number.* God is always
   more concerned about the attitude of our hearts
   than about the amount we place in the offering
   plate. This is not an excuse to minimize our
   generosity; it's an encouragement to focus less on
   the number and more on the motivation behind
   the number. God doesn't want "generosity" that
   is driven by legalism or guilt; he wants us to give
   freely out of our love and gratitude for him.

2. *God doesn't ask us to steward what he hasn't provided.*
   Throughout our lives, there will be seasons when
   God provides much and seasons when God
   provides less. We are told to steward well the
   resources he has provided.

3. *We are to give proportionally.* If we're in a season
   when God is providing fewer resources, that's okay.
   We can't give what God hasn't given us, but we
   can give generously in proportion to what he has
   provided. When our income is reduced, the amount
   we give may change, but the proportion may stay
   the same.

4. *Be prayerful.* Could God impress upon our hearts
   to keep giving at the same level even as our income
   decreases? Absolutely. But that decision should be
   the result of our prayerfully seeking God's desire
   for our generosity. The starting point for any giving

decision is *prayer*, seeking out what God would have us do.

I didn't tell Jacob that he should reduce his generosity. But I also didn't tell him he should keep giving the same amount. It wasn't my place to make such a decision. I did, however, discuss what God reveals in Scripture and encouraged Jacob and his wife to seek God's guidance for their giving.

Is it wrong to reduce our giving when our resources are reduced? No. That may be part of what God wanted Jacob to learn. He may have been using that moment to teach Jacob that generosity is not about a specific number. I don't know. But whatever the decision, it must be the result of prayer and seeking God's guidance and direction.

ABOVE AND BEYOND GIVING

Ten percent of our gross income is a good starting point for giving. But what should we do if we're already giving 10 percent of our gross income? Do we give beyond that mark?

Though we find the 10 percent standard used in the Old Testament, we also find examples of men and women going well beyond the tithe in both the Old and New Testaments.

Consider what Paul says about the Macedonians in 2 Corinthians 8:3-5: "I can testify that they gave not only what they could afford, but far more. And they did it of their own free will. They begged us again and again for the privilege of sharing in the gift for the believers in Jerusalem. They even did more than we had hoped, for their first action was to give themselves to the Lord and to us, just as God wanted them to do."

The Macedonians considered it an honor to participate in the mission of God. They could not think of a better way to leverage their resources. For them, everything was on the table. Even the little bit they had was held with open hands.

So, what should we do when we hit the 10 percent mark? Prayerfully explore ways that we can continue to live and give generously.

Maybe you feel God prompting you to give more. If so, ask yourself the following questions as you consider giving above and beyond the tithe:

- *Should I give more to my church?* The church is God's plan to reach the world. The church builds disciples, helps the hurting, spreads the gospel, and sends missionaries around the world. What an amazing opportunity to participate in God's mission. Should you increase the amount you give to your church?
- *Should I give to another Kingdom-advancing, nonprofit ministry?* God is doing great things in and through many nonprofit organizations. They take care of orphans, feed the hungry, and help send missionaries

around the world. Should you support one of these ministries?

- *Should I set aside money for others' unforeseen needs?* Setting aside some resources prepares you to be ready to give when opportunities arise. In a sense, you are planning for the financial needs of others, and you are ready to meet the needs that God places before you. Maybe you buy groceries for someone who just lost their job. Maybe you help pay someone's utility bill during a colder-than-normal winter. What an amazing way to show people the love of God by meeting their immediate needs.

Maybe you could do all three, putting a little toward each option. Though I certainly recommend giving your first 10 percent to the church, you can be more flexible with the rest. All are good options. So prayerfully consider how God would want you to use your "above and beyond" giving.

God is the Creator and owner of all things. His resources are abundant and never-ending. Let's follow God's lead and give in proportion to what we have received.

WHERE DO YOU GO FROM HERE?

1. Read 2 Corinthians 9:11. How does this verse relate to proportional giving? What should happen when God entrusts us with greater income?

2. Why do some people hesitate to increase their generosity as their income increases?

3. Prior to reading this chapter, how did you view tithing? How do you view it now? What changes will you make in your giving as a result?

4. Spend some time prayerfully seeking the proportion that God desires you to give. Write it down and commit to it.

10

GIVING SACRIFICIALLY

Jeremy was the pastor of a church in the heart of downtown Las Vegas. At Christmastime, the church decided to hold a holiday brunch. Though the food was good and the fellowship was enjoyable, it was a widow who caught Jeremy's attention the most.

Jeremy knew her. She was a recovering addict and had a son who was significantly struggling. Financially, every month was a challenge for her. She had very little income and was living on food stamps.

But she loved Jesus.

When she heard about the Christmas brunch, she not only wanted to attend but also desired to help with the brunch.

No one expected anything of her, but when she walked into the room on the day of the brunch, she was carrying a casserole. Jeremy knew what that casserole meant. She had forgone the opportunity to use her food stamps on herself and instead bought the ingredients to provide food for others.

She ate less so others could eat more.

And she wouldn't have wanted it any other way. She was overjoyed to have the opportunity to contribute.

She gave sacrificially, which is exactly what eternity-shaping givers do. They remember the sacrifice of Jesus, that "he humbled himself in obedience to God and died a criminal's death on a cross" (Philippians 2:8). They let his sacrifice guide their sacrifice.

UNCOMFORTABLE, SACRIFICIAL GENEROSITY

A sacrifice is a need or want given up for the sake of someone else.

In the United States, we like to be comfortable. We chase after a better house, a better car, a full retirement account. We avoid pain and pursue comfort.

But biblical generosity is not comfortable generosity. It isn't comfortable because biblical generosity is not about the leftovers. When we make generosity a priority, we intentionally forgo our wants—and, sometimes, our needs.

And that's uncomfortable. However, this sacrificial generosity is exactly what we find in Scripture.

I already told you the story of the widow in Las Vegas. Let me tell you about another widow, this one in Jerusalem.

In Mark 12:41-44, we find Jesus and his disciples outside the Temple treasury, the place where people delivered their gifts to God. Jesus watched as the wealthy brought their large gifts to the treasury. The disciples may have been watching the scene as well.

Using some imagination, you can hear the disciples pointing out those who were giving large gifts:

"Look at him! He must really love God."

"Did you see what that guy gave? Wow. God must be really pleased with him."

"That was an incredible gift. God is going to do big things with that amount of money."

Then Jesus called the disciples over.

Was he going to laud and celebrate the large gifts given by the rich? Was he going to tell the disciples that the gifts of the wealthy were indicators of their love for God? Was he going to tell them that, because these large gifts were provided, God was finally able to do something truly significant?

Not at all.

There was a person he wanted them to see that no one else had noticed.

While the wealthy were giving their large gifts, a widow

had stepped onto the scene. From the standpoint of wealth, she had very little to give—only two small coins. The amount would not have impressed anyone in the Temple treasury that day. She wouldn't have been invited to a donor event. She wouldn't have received a call from the religious leaders, thanking her for being so generous. She wouldn't even have received a handwritten thank-you note.

She wasn't worth their time.

No one noticed her.

Except Jesus.

Jesus knew something about this woman that others did not. Not only did he know how much money was in her hand, he knew how much money was left at home. This woman's gift represented everything she had.

Jesus also knew something about the wealthy that others did not. They were giving out of their excess. Their gifts were comfortable. They would return home, and life would be no different than when they left.

The widow's gift was uncomfortable. She would return home and life would be significantly different.

You see, in God's economy, the amount sacrificed always supersedes the amount given. God is not nearly as concerned about what is placed in the offering plate as he is with what is left in the bank account.

King David understood this. In 2 Samuel 24:24, when someone tries to give David the property and animals necessary for his sacrifice, David replies, "No, I insist on buying it, for I will not present burnt offerings to the Lord my God that have cost me nothing."

Abraham was willing to offer up his son, Isaac, as a sacrifice to God.

The widow in 1 Kings 17 provided Elijah with water and bread before making bread for herself and her son, even when she thought it would be their last meal.

Uncomfortable.

Sacrificial.

The generosity we find in the Bible is not easy. It is not convenient. And it is certainly not comfortable. Sacrifice is uncomfortable. The generosity we are called to in the Bible causes our hearts to lean into God and trust him.

THE DANGERS OF A SCARCITY MINDSET

What hinders sacrificial generosity? There are several possible hinderances, such as placing our hope in comfort and material wealth. But I want to focus on one obstacle in particular: a scarcity mindset. God and his resources are unlimited. But those with a scarcity mindset do not live or give accordingly.

A scarcity mindset is built on the belief that there is not enough to go around and that God's provision will come up short. Someone will be left out. Those with a scarcity mindset believe that resources are finite and therefore we must fight to get our slice of the limited pie and hold on tightly to what we have.

There are dangers related to a scarcity mindset.

1. *A scarcity mindset creates bitterness.* With a scarcity mindset, we find it very difficult to be happy when someone else experiences an increase. And though we may never admit it, we're happy when someone else's resources decrease.

   Why? Because with a scarcity mindset, the only way to gain is for someone else to lose.

2. *A scarcity mindset leads to envy.* When we have a scarcity mindset, envy of others cannot be far behind. We want what another person has and wonder why we can't have it. Why didn't we get the new car? Why didn't we get the big house? Why didn't we get the promotion?

3. *A scarcity mindset causes us to be self-reliant instead of relying on God.* When we believe that God's resources are limited, we're tempted to rely on our own strength to get whatever we can. We trust in our own efforts and assume that any increase in resources is the result of our hard work, not God's grace.

4. *A scarcity mindset makes us act as if God's love is meager and limited.* With a scarcity mindset, we

start to believe that God's provision of material resources is a measure of his love for us. Likewise, we believe that an absence of resources means that God doesn't care about us.

5. *A scarcity mindset leads to hoarding.* With a scarcity mindset, we do not give sacrificially. We do not believe God has the resources to provide all that we need. We act like doomsday preppers—hoarding our resources instead of releasing them to help others.

Sacrificial giving requires us to trust that God is not limited, and neither are his resources. He can provide whatever he wants whenever he wants. What he provides is just another way of forming our hearts to be more like his. Our hearts are infinitely more important to him than the type of car we drive, house we live in, or balance in our bank account.

God can and will use his abundant resources to shape our hearts and glorify his name.

IS THE SACRIFICE WORTH IT?

We are willing to sacrifice our money, time, energy, and other resources for our family, friends, work, and church because we believe the outcome is worth it.

And so it is with sacrificial giving. When we give sacrificially, we are saying *no* to one thing so we can say *yes* to something of greater value.

Why would we give sacrificially? Why would we let go of something important or valuable? Why would we enter the realm of uncomfortable giving?

We must first believe that the reward is worth the sacrifice.

Do you believe the gospel is worth sacrificing for?

Do you believe seeing lives transformed in your community and around the world is worth it?

Do you believe placing your trust in God is worth it?

Do you believe your heart is worth it?

If you believe the sacrifice is worth the outcome, you will find that a lack of comfort can truly become a wealth of cheer. A sacrificial heart is a satisfied heart.

God set the standard for sacrificial giving when he sent his one and only Son, Jesus, into the world. While on earth, Jesus lived a sinless life, doing what no other human could ever do. Yet he was condemned to die a sinner's death. Jesus willingly hung on the cross, knowing that his sacrifice was the only way that we could ever be forgiven for our sins and have our relationship with God restored.

There will never be a greater sacrifice.

Will you follow Christ's lead? The sacrifice is worth it.

WHERE DO YOU GO FROM HERE?

1. Read Mark 12:41-44. What stands out to you in the story of the poor widow?

2. Why do you think God delights in sacrificial giving rather than comfortable giving?

3. What concerns do you have about sacrificial generosity? How do you hope to see God work through your sacrificial generosity?

4. For Kingdom-minded givers, the question is not, "Does God want me to sacrifice?" but, "*What* does God want me to sacrifice?" Pray that God will reveal to you the sacrifices he wants you to make. Write down what he impresses on your heart.

11

GIVING CHEERFULLY

Ray and Krystal were broke, but after listening to their pastor teach on biblical generosity, they decided to trust God and start giving.

With their car's fuel gauge on empty, they coasted on fumes into the church parking lot the next Sunday.

They had only twenty dollars between them.

Could they have used that money for gas? Sure. But they were determined to put God first in their finances.

During the service, when the offering was passed, Ray placed the twenty dollars into the plate. He and his wife now had nothing, but they were trusting God.

When the service ended, the couple walked toward the rear exit, hoping their car would make it home without running out of gas. Before they could make it out of the worship center, an elderly woman walked up to them. To their utter disbelief, she told them that God wanted her to give them some money.

Ray and Krystal politely refused the gift. They didn't feel right taking money from an elderly woman.

But the woman was determined. She said that God had convinced her to give the young couple some money, and if they didn't take it, they were denying her a blessing and causing her to be disobedient.

I can imagine her saying these things in a gentle tone and with a smile on her face.

Ray and Krystal did the only thing they felt they could do. They agreed to take the money.

As the elderly lady laid some cash in Ray's hand, he looked down at the bills. She had given him one hundred dollars.

The couple thanked the woman and continued out to their car. Once they were inside, they looked at each other, cried, and thanked God for his provision.

There are at least two lessons in this story. One is a lesson of trusting in God's provision, being obedient when obedience is not easy. In this case, provision came in the form of needed financial resources.

The second lesson is one of cheerful generosity. God impressed on the elderly woman that she should give to the young couple. And not only did she give as God had prompted her, but she gave eagerly and cheerfully. The only time she grew concerned about the gift was when the couple tried to refuse it.

This is what eternity-shaping givers do. They give cheerfully.

SMILE

Imagine if one of my sons presented me with a gift but didn't seem excited to give it to me. What if he was noticeably irritated? His countenance was bitter. His words were forced. I would probably surmise that the gift was given out of obligation. His mom made him do it.

How do you think I would respond?

I might say, "I love you, son, but maybe you should keep the gift. I really don't want a gift that is given grudgingly."

God feels the same way. He doesn't want a bunch of guilt-driven, reluctant, grumpy givers. The giver's attitude matters to God. With God, it's all about the heart.

In 2 Corinthians 9:7, it says, "You must each decide in your heart how much to give. And don't give reluctantly or in response to pressure. 'For God loves a person who gives cheerfully.'"

Paul wrote these words right after he told the Corinthians about the generosity of the Macedonians.

The Macedonians were experiencing significant suffering

and deep poverty. But they were passionate about the things of God. They were moved by what moves God, and they recognized an opportunity to participate in what God was doing.

So even though they were poor, they gave generously to help the church in Jerusalem. Paul tells the extent of their generosity:

> I can testify that they gave not only what they could afford, but far more. And they did it of their own free will. They begged us again and again for the privilege of sharing in the gift for the believers in Jerusalem.
>
> 2 CORINTHIANS 8:3-4

That's crazy. They gave beyond what they could afford and were begging Paul to allow them to give even more. They considered giving for the sake of the gospel to be an honor and a privilege. They were eager and cheerful givers.

When I was growing up, the image in my mind of the widow in Mark 12 who gave the two coins was completely wrong. Whenever the story of the widow's mite was told in Sunday school, they used a picture of an elderly, sad, hunched over woman. I assume this was to communicate her struggle. So every time I read Mark 12, I imagined a miserable-looking woman. And I felt bad for her.

But then something clicked.

God desires cheerful givers. So why would Jesus point out a miserable woman to illustrate real generosity?

Now I picture her in a completely different way. There's no way she was a grumpy giver. More likely, she had the biggest and most contagious smile in the entire Temple. She effused lightheartedness as she deposited her two coins. She was more than happy to give what she had to the Temple treasury. Giving was not a burden for her. Like the Macedonians, she considered it an honor and privilege to give out of her poverty.

This is the type of giver God desires. He wants gifts from those who give out of love for him and his mission. He wants gifts from those who consider it an honor and privilege to give. He wants gifts from givers with massive grins across their faces.

The money matters little to God. It's all his anyway. What matters is the heart of the giver.

GRUMPY OR CHEERFUL GIVING?

How can you distinguish a grumpy giver from a cheerful one? Both may contribute to their local church, but they are very different from one another. Using the Macedonians as our guide, here are some common differences.

Mine or his?

Grumpy givers act as if what they have is truly their own. Consequently, they become attached to and proud of their possessions. When they give, it feels like giving away a part of themselves.

Cheerful givers hold their possessions loosely. They recognize that everything belongs to God and they are managers or stewards, not owners. Giving is enjoyable because they see how resources under their management become deployed for Kingdom purposes—which is the goal.

Legalism and guilt or love and opportunity?

Grumpy givers just want to check the box to meet their obligation. They view generosity as one more hoop to jump through as a Christian. Giving is not something they look forward to. They feel guilty if they don't give, so they give. But not without hesitation.

Cheerful givers can't wait to give. They give because they are grateful for God's generosity to them. And they are passionate about others getting to know the love of God as well. They cherish the opportunity to participate in God's mission.

Our agenda or God's agenda?

Grumpy givers like to provide instructions for how their dollars can be used. Often, the instructions ensure that they somehow benefit from their gift. After all, if they're going to give, they might as well get something out it.

Cheerful givers want their gifts to be used by God to maximize his glory and advance his Kingdom. They are not unwise or wasteful givers, but they are not controlling givers either. They just want their gifts to be used for Kingdom purposes.

Giving the bare minimum or giving sacrificially?

Grumpy givers often give from their surplus. Even if they give 10 percent, they have become so accustomed to that amount that they barely think about it. They just want to make sure they can say, "Yes, I tithe."

Cheerful givers are very prayerful and thoughtful when it comes to generosity. Giving stretches their faith. When they give, they intentionally lay aside other wants and desires to make the gift. They feel their generosity.

IT IS BETTER TO GIVE THAN TO GET

In Acts 20:35, Paul encourages the Ephesian elders to help the weak and "remember the words of the Lord Jesus: 'It is more blessed to give than to receive.'"

In God's economy, giving is better than getting. Understanding this truth can produce cheerful giving.

- When we *give*, we loosen the grip of materialism. The Bible says we cannot serve both God and money (Matthew 6:24). Giving loosens our grip on this world and tightens our grip on eternity.
- When we *give*, we are less stressed. Generosity demonstrates that we have put our hope in a God who will not fail us. Those who put their hope in money and possessions will find their hope fluctuating along with the stock market.
- When we *give*, we find greater contentment. First Timothy 6:19 says that in giving we find "life that is truly life" (NIV). In other words, generosity allows us to experience the present blessings of God—such as contentment and satisfaction—regardless of how many possessions we have.
- When we *give*, we get to participate in changing people's lives. God uses our resources to do amazing things through the church. Our generosity can be a part of healing broken marriages, feeding the hungry, and reaching the lost in our community and around the world. What a privilege.
- When we *give*, our hearts become more committed to the mission of the church. Mathew 6:21 tells us that our heart follows our treasure. Where we give, our heart goes. When we give to our local church and its

Kingdom-advancing ministry, we will find ourselves more engaged and committed.

- When we *give*, our confidence in God's promises and provision grows. We see how God generously provides for our needs. We see how God makes us "enriched in every way" (2 Corinthians 9:11). Those who give will see God fulfill his promises, which only increases their trust in him.

It is truly better to give than to get. The cheerful giver's heart experiences this truth. This is why generous givers are happy givers.

CHEERFUL SACRIFICE

In the previous chapter, we saw that giving should be sacrificial. In this chapter, we've seen that God desires cheerful givers. On the surface, these two principles of giving seem to contradict one another. How can we be cheerful in the midst of sacrifice?

God shows us.

Isaiah 53:10 says, "It was the LORD's good plan to crush him and cause him grief. Yet when his life is made an offering for sin, he will have many descendants."

God was pleased by the sacrifice of Jesus. It was a part

of his "good plan." Though the sacrifice was great, God still gave cheerfully.

How?

He looked through the lens of eternity and saw the worthy outcome. He saw many descendants. He saw you and me in relationship with him.

So how do we reconcile significant sacrifice and cheerfulness? How do we find joy during uncomfortable generosity? We consider those lives that will be changed for all eternity, those who will hear the gospel and put their faith in Christ because of our generosity.

Smile as you give. God is using your generosity to change lives.

WHERE DO YOU GO FROM HERE?

1. What would it be like to receive a gift that was begrudgingly given?

2. Read 2 Corinthians 9:7. Why do some people give begrudging gifts to the church?

3. What does cheerful giving communicate to those who have yet to put their faith in Christ?

4. Pray that God will give you a heart like that of the Macedonians. Pray that God will develop in you a heart that is cheerfully eager to give.

12

PRIORITIZING THE LOCAL CHURCH

Dennis is the senior pastor of a midsize church in the St. Louis area. Recently, the couple who had run their premarital counseling program moved to another state. This was a significant loss because the church had three couples who needed to go through premarital counseling before their rapidly approaching wedding dates arrived.

When it was suggested that the Smiths take over the ministry, Dennis could not think of a better couple. They had been part of the church for a few years, seemed to have a strong marriage, and had a counseling background.

Problem solved, Dennis thought.

But the problem wasn't solved. In fact, a new problem

was introduced. The church required all volunteer leaders to demonstrate regular giving to the church. There wasn't a particular amount they looked for, just a demonstration of consistent financial generosity.

When the Smiths' giving records were pulled, Dennis was shocked. There was nothing. The Smiths had never given to the church.

"That's not possible," Dennis said.

But it was. The Smiths later confirmed they had never given to the church.

But why? And how? Dennis wondered. *And who else?*

The fact that some regular attendees do not financially support the church can surprise the leaders. But the reality is more common than one might think.

Men and women who view money in light of eternity follow Jesus in prioritizing the church, for which he willingly gave his life. But many others do not.

WHY PEOPLE DON'T GIVE TO THEIR CHURCH

There are many in the church who give very little compared to what God has given them. Or maybe they don't give at all. I have seen the giving numbers from numerous churches. The reality for many, if not most churches, is that they are financially sustained by a relatively small group in the congregation.

Why do so many people who attend church not give? The potential causes are numerous and often complex. But allow me to highlight four common reasons I've run across.

They don't know they're supposed to give

In previous generations, church attendance and giving to the church were part of being a good citizen of the community. It was expected. If you didn't attend church and put money in the offering plate, eyebrows were raised.

"What's wrong with that guy?"

Additionally, children in previous generations saw their parents put money in the offering plate or box every Sunday. They learned by observation.

But things have changed.

Gone are the days when attending and giving to a church are expected of good community members. In some areas, identifying with a local church may even hurt one's status.

And gone are the days when kids learn to give by watching their parents. For many families, online giving has eliminated the public giving of an offering. If parents don't tell their children that they give online, the kids may never know that Mom and Dad support the local church financially.

Church leaders cannot assume that attendees know what the Bible teaches about generosity. The primary way that most people know what God says about money and generosity is by the teaching of God's Word in the church.

They don't make giving a priority

Finances are tight. There are too many bills and too little money in the bank account. Sometimes the absence of financial margin is self-inflicted. A string of bad financial decisions has created a burden of debt. Sometimes the cause is external, such as a medical emergency or a car that breaks down. Regardless, many people wait until their bills and wants are covered before they give to their local church, putting their faith in themselves rather than in God.

They felt burned by a previous church

Bad church experiences can happen, and some people's prior experiences have made them skeptical of church leadership in general. Maybe they went to a church where the pastor used the pulpit for personal gain. Maybe they went to a church where financial accountability and security were lax. Maybe they attended a church with rampant poor stewardship.

Whatever happened, their experience affects their current perception and practice. They may feel that church leadership can't be trusted to use money wisely. They may think they can make better stewardship decisions. They may give to other organizations, but they don't give to the church.

They don't understand the importance of the local church

There are many who fit into this category. They go to church because "that's what good Christians do." They are often very detached from the church, attending a service and leaving quickly. They've checked the box.

They don't understand how the church fits into God's plan. They don't see how the church is so much more than a weekly service to attend. They miss that God is using the church they attend to eternally affect lives in their community and around the world.

GOD'S PLAN TO REACH THE WORLD

Do you understand the importance of the local church? Maybe you've attended church all your life, or maybe you're new to the faith, but has anyone ever taught you why the church is important? Or do you just show up on Sunday morning because that's what you have always done or have seen Christians do?

Have you ever stopped long enough to ask *why* you should show up? And *why* you should give specifically to the local church?

The church was God's idea, not a human invention. God created the church for five essential purposes: worship and prayer, edification, discipleship, evangelism, and fellowship.[7] When the church does these things well, it brings glory to God. Let's explore this in greater detail.

1. *The church glorifies God through worship and prayer.*
   We've already defined *worship* as ascribing worth
   to something. God created the church so that,
   individually and collectively, we can show honor
   and reverence for him through music, the reading
   and exposition of Scripture, generous giving,
   baptism, and the Lord's Supper. Our worship
   praises God and encourages others in the faith.
   And through our worship and prayer, God is
   glorified.

2. *The church glorifies God through edification.* To
   edify means to instruct or improve someone. As
   Christians, we want our hearts to reflect God's
   heart. When we gather as a local church, God
   teaches us through his Word how to align our will
   with his and become more like Jesus. Teaching can
   occur in the main service or in smaller, classroom-
   like settings. Through our edification, God is
   glorified.

3. *The church glorifies God through discipleship.*
   Discipleship is the ongoing process of developing
   followers of Jesus. Incorporating teaching,
   accountability, and encouragement, discipleship is
   the means of multiplying and maturing followers of
   Jesus. Disciples make disciples who make disciples.
   And through our discipleship, God is glorified.

4. *The church glorifies God through evangelism.*
   Evangelism is the spreading of the gospel. God
   did not create the church to be a holy huddle,
   focused solely on the needs of its members. It is
   not a country club for nice people. God created the
   church to get the news of Jesus out to the ends of
   the earth. We gather as a local church to learn about
   and become more like Jesus so we can go and tell
   others about the hope we have. We gather together
   to go and tell. And through our evangelism, God is
   glorified.

5. *The church glorifies God through fellowship.* God
   doesn't want a bunch of Lone Ranger Christians.
   We are meant to share life with one another. Our
   common bond with Christ creates spiritually
   founded relationships that spur one another on in
   the faith. So we gather to fellowship. And through
   our fellowship, God is glorified.

The potential impact of the local church cannot be over-stated, though its power is often overlooked by church members. God's plan is to use the local church to change the world and shape eternity.

Have new believers put their faith in Jesus? Have broken marriages become whole again? Have the hungry been fed? Have the homeless received shelter? Have needy children received school supplies? Do parents better understand how to raise their children? Have babies been adopted? Have foster children slept soundly in a bed for the first time in years?

Because of the local church, the answer to these questions is often *yes*. Through the local church, the lonely find friends, doubters find answers, the lost are found, and the broken are put back together.

God works through local churches to change communities and the world. He uses local churches to form hearts that look more like his. We may not always hear the stories, but we can be certain that God is working through the local church, taking our gifts of money, time, and attention and multiplying them in ways that only he can.

WHERE TO GIVE WHEN YOU ARE IN BETWEEN CHURCHES

Perhaps as you read this, you are in between churches. Maybe you recently moved to a new city. Maybe something unfortunate happened at your previous church. Whatever the reason, you have left the church you were part of and are searching for another one. You still find yourself desiring to financially participate in God's mission by giving to the local church, but you are not sure where to give.

I've been there. When my wife and I moved from Florida to North Carolina, we took the first few months in our new city to visit several churches. Since we were not tied to any church at the time, we discussed how and where we should give.

Here are some options we considered. They may help you during your time of transition.

1. *Keep giving to your former church.* We loved our former church and continued to be grateful for their ministry. Consider giving to your former church until you settle on a new church.

2. *Give to the churches you visit.* The churches we visited were likely making a significant impact in their community. Consider giving to each church you attend during your transition.

3. *Give to a church in financial need.* Many churches struggle financially. Sometimes they face financial challenges not because of anything they did, but simply because of their location. Maybe they minister to a rural or low-income community. Consider identifying one of these churches and sending your gifts to them.

4. *Give to a Kingdom-advancing nonprofit organization.* God works through many different ministries outside the local church. Perhaps you already donate to some Kingdom-advancing ministries. During your transitional period, consider increasing your generosity to them.

5. *Set aside your gifts until you find a new church.*
   You could earmark your gifts for the church you
   eventually decide to join. This is my least favorite
   option because it breaks the pattern of regular
   giving and could tempt us to use the money for
   other purposes.

The only option we did not consider was taking a break
from giving and using those funds for personal needs or
wants.

In our case, my wife and I decided to continue giving to
our former church until we found a congregation to join in
our new community.

What should you do? Seek God in prayer and see where
he leads you. Just make sure you continue to give proportionally, sacrificially, and cheerfully.

LET YOUR HEART FOLLOW YOUR MONEY

Maybe you find it hard to get excited about giving to your
local church because you don't feel connected. Here's my suggestion: Start giving and let your heart follow your money.

As Jesus says in Matthew 6:21, "Wherever your treasure
is, there the desires of your heart will also be."

Notice that he doesn't say, "Give to where your heart is."
No, wherever your money goes, your heart will follow.

Whenever you financially invest in something, you start paying attention to it. You care more about it because now you have some skin in the game. Once you begin giving to your local church, you will pay more attention to it. You will feel more connected to it. You will become more excited about how God is using it.

Those who place their money in possessions will care about possessions.

Those who place their money in their children's athletics will care about their children's athletics.

Those who give their money to a nonprofit organization will care about that organization.

Those who invest their money in the church will care about the church.

That's how God wired our hearts. We care about the things we're invested in.

Start giving to your local church and let your heart follow.

1. Why do you think some people don't give to their church?

2. Read Ephesians 3:10, Acts 2:42, and Hebrews 10:25. What stands out to you about the local church in these passages?

3. How have you seen God use your church to have an impact on individuals and your community?

4. Pray that God will deepen your love for his church, the church that he sent Jesus to die for.

13

ENCOURAGING OTHERS
TO GIVE

"Why don't we just talk about it?"

Jeff's question caught everyone off guard.

According to their giving numbers, the percentage of givers in the church had decreased over the past couple of years.

The percentage decrease was the result of something good that was happening in the church: More people were attending. The church was reaching more people than ever, but many of the new attendees were not giving.

So the pastor gathered a few of the church's small group leaders to discuss what they should do. Jeff was one of them. He was in his early seventies but always had a youthful smile.

"We can't just talk about giving," replied Aaron. "If I talk about generosity in my small group, people will get uncomfortable. They'll probably leave."

"That hasn't been my experience," said Jeff with his usual grin. "I've been talking about it to my small group for a while. I bet every one of them gives now. And most of them have thanked me for it."

The room was quiet.

Jeff broke the silence. "Look, why would we not encourage others to do something that brings us so much happiness? Those who don't give are missing out on God's blessings. Knowing what I know, experiencing what I've experienced, how can I withhold this from them?"

The room was quiet again.

Jeff continued, "I don't talk about generosity because I want our church to meet budget or because I want our numbers to look good. I encourage others to be generous because I love them and want them to experience what God has for them. They see my genuine contentment and that I'm not always chasing a higher standard of living. They want to know where that comes from. So I tell them."

Those in the room were beginning to nod their heads in agreement.

Jeff added one more comment: "Generosity is just too good to keep secret."

Eternity-shaping givers know the truth of Jeff's words.

WHAT CONTAGIOUS GENEROSITY LOOKS LIKE

As a dad of three boys, I know what *contagious* means. I've seen viruses go from one child to the next with little effort. The other brothers simply need to be around the sick brother to catch whatever he has. Sometimes it seems as if they catch the same virus multiple times.

I guess you could say they are overachievers.

Most of the time when we hear the word *contagious*, we think "not good." But not everything that's contagious is bad. There are some things we hope other people will catch quickly.

Generosity is one of those things.

By modeling generous giving, we encourage others to give as well. We hope they will see the benefits of generosity in our lives and say, "I want that."

As we have seen, God promises blessing and provision when we give. The blessings can be physical gain, spiritual gain, or both. These blessings can be seen by others and may prompt them to live with open hands as well. These blessings can cause the desire for generous living to move from one person to the next.

It's contagious.

Contagious generosity shows itself in contentment. In a world perpetually chasing the next rung on the materialism ladder, seeing someone who is content is rare and refreshing. Others want it.

It's contagious.

Contagious generosity looks like an adventurous life. Building a self-centered kingdom leads to regular bouts of boredom and chasing the next great disappointment. God orchestrates lives for the generous that they could never have planned on their own—lives that advance God's Kingdom in remarkable ways. Those who view money in the light of eternity see firsthand the power of God in their lives. Others want the same.

It's contagious.

Contagious generosity looks like deep relationships. You rarely meet someone who is both generous and lonely. Those who live with open hands tend to develop deep relationships because they are the ones who help in times of need and lay themselves down for other people. Others see these genuine relationships and want the same.

It's contagious.

Contagious generosity looks like provision. God promises to meet the needs of those who give and trust him with their resources. Those whose generosity aligns with what we find in the Bible will find God's promise of provision to be true. Others notice and want it as well.

It's contagious.

As God makes good on his promises to generous givers, generosity spreads, infecting others. But this is not the only way generous givers encourage generosity. They also use their words to spur on others to live generously.

GENEROSITY IS TOO GOOD TO KEEP SECRET

"I don't talk about or encourage a person to give generously because giving is a private matter between God and the individual. It's not my place."

I've heard statements like this for many years. In the past, I may have even said something similar.

This line of thinking is often rooted in one's interpretation of Matthew 6:1-4.

Watch out! Don't do your good deeds publicly, to be admired by others, for you will lose the reward from your Father in heaven. When you give to someone in need, don't do as the hypocrites do—blowing trumpets in the synagogues and streets to call attention to their acts of charity! I tell you the truth, they have received all the reward they will ever get. But when you give to someone in need, don't let your left hand know what your right hand is doing. Give your gifts in private, and your Father, who sees everything, will reward you.

It's the last part that leads some people to think that giving is not something we should discuss or address. But before you come to the same conclusion, allow me to point out a few things.

In this passage, Jesus is addressing the issue of religious hypocrisy. Some people were turning their giving into a spectacle, making a big to-do about their generosity. They made sure everyone knew when they were giving.

Jesus makes the same point about their prayer and fasting.

The key to understanding this passage is their motivation: "to be admired by others."

These religious grandstanders prayed, fasted, and gave in a manner that drew attention and praise to themselves. Their actions were not about their love for God but their love for themselves. In their hearts, they were seeking earthly rewards. They wanted others to be in awe of them.

When it says in Matthew 6:6, "When you pray, go away by yourself, shut the door behind you, and pray to your Father in private," it doesn't mean we should not talk about, ask about, or encourage prayer. Your pastor isn't sinning when he publicly prays during a church service. We aren't sinning when we pray over a meal. And we're not wrong for asking other believers about their prayer life.

Similarly, Jesus isn't saying that generosity is an off-limits topic of conversation. Instead, he is challenging his listeners to consider their motivations and heart.

Jesus regularly talked about and encouraged generosity. Paul regularly talked about and encouraged generosity. The New Testament church knew who gave.

The Bible is clear: We can and should feel comfortable

talking about, asking about, and encouraging generosity. But we shouldn't pour on guilt or be legalistic. Just as God doesn't want generosity motivated by self-glorification, he doesn't want generosity motivated by guilt or legalism.

We encourage generosity because we don't want others to miss out on what God has in store for them when they give. We want everyone to "experience true life" (1 Timothy 6:19)—a life marked by the present blessings of God.

INVITING OTHERS INTO THE JOY OF GENEROSITY

Over many years, I have seen eternity-shaping givers invite others into the joy of generosity. For people like Jeff, it is a natural overflow of their generosity as they desire to help others grasp the blessings of God. Inviting others into the joy of generosity is simply another indicator of a generous heart.

How do eternity-shaping givers spread the generosity bug?

- *They genuinely care about others.* They are less concerned about the church meeting its budget than seeing church members' hearts reflect the heart of God. They want to see people align themselves with God's design for money and generosity.
- *They invite others into their own generosity journey.* Eternity-shaping givers are excited to tell their own

generosity story. They weren't always openhanded. Many have a stingy past. But they love telling others how God molded a generous heart into them over the years. Occasionally, they will invite others to join them in giving their time, talent, or treasure as a first step toward living generously.

- *They celebrate what God does through the church.* They love watching God work through the church. They ask, "Did you see what God did?" And they are ready with a story about God's faithfulness and provision. They celebrate the church's impact because it demonstrates how God multiplies our resources to advance his Kingdom.

- *They talk about God's design for money.* Eternity-shaping givers are not afraid to talk about money. They understand what Scripture teaches about a variety of money topics—debt, savings, paying bills, and, of course, generosity. Generous givers know that poor financial decisions can hinder generosity.

- *They talk about the generosity of others.* They won't brag about their own generosity, but they will talk about the generosity of others. They love to celebrate followers of Jesus who take steps of faith with their resources. They find generosity inspiring. So when they see others giving generously, they talk about it.

Inviting others into the joy of generosity is not difficult. It takes a love for others and some intentionality. Consider how you might encourage others to pursue a life marked by generosity as you do the same.

WHERE DO YOU GO FROM HERE?

1. Read 2 Corinthians 8 and 9. What stands out to you about Paul's encouragement of generosity?

2. Has anyone encouraged or inspired you to live generously? How did this person make you want to be more generous?

3. What steps can you take to encourage someone else to live generously?

4. Pray that God will help you encourage others to be generous with the resources God has provided them.

THIS BOOK IS NOT ULTIMATELY ABOUT MONEY

Though we have discussed money and generosity at length, they are not what this book is ultimately about. The message is more about your heart—your attitudes, your perspective, your focus in life. God addresses money and generosity, not because he needs a handout, but because he wants your wholehearted participation in his mission on Earth.

Aligning yourself with God's design for money and generosity will shape your heart to be more like his. God desires your heart, and your heart naturally desires God and his blessings. Generous giving is a way for you to experience the very things for which your heart longs.

But it's not just about *your* heart. It's also about the hearts of others.

Your generosity can contribute to changing another person's heart for eternity. God can use your generosity to reach someone who has yet to receive Christ as Savior.

Your generosity can also inspire other believers to stop chasing after the wind—those things that will never fulfill us—and live with open hands. And their hearts will become more like God's heart as well.

Your generosity matters on an eternal level—changing your heart and the hearts of others.

What an opportunity. What an honor.

View your money in the light of eternity.

Give generously.

ABOUT THE AUTHOR

Art Rainer is the founder of Christian Money Solutions. He writes and speaks widely about issues related to finance, wealth, and generosity. He is the author of *The Money Challenge: 30 Days of Discovering God's Design for You and Your Money*. You can read and hear more from Art at ArtRainer.com.

NOTES

1. Elizabeth. W. Dunn, Lara B. Aknin, and Michael I. Norton, "Prosocial Spending and Happiness: Using Money to Benefit Others Pays Off," *Current Directions in Psychological Science*, vol. 23, no. 1 (February 2014), 41–47.

2. Lara B. Aknin, et al., "Prosocial Spending and Well-Being: Cross-Cultural Evidence for a Psychological Universal, *Journal of Personality and Social Psychology*, vol. 104, no. 4 (April 2013), 635.

3. Mark Hall, "The Greatest Wealth Transfer in History: What's Happening and What Are the Implications," *Forbes*, November 11, 2019.

4. James D. Wise *Inheritolatry: The Final Obstacle to Completing the Great Commission* (Maitland, FL: Xulon, 2017), xi.

5. Wise, xiii.

6. Randy Alcorn, *The Treasure Principle: Unlocking the Secret of Joyful Giving* (Colorado Springs: Multnomah, 2001), 41.

7. Aspects of this discussion are drawn from Thom S. Rainer, *Surprising Insights from the Unchurched and Proven Ways to Reach Them* (Grand Rapids, MI: Zondervan, 2008), 122; and Mark Dever, *The Church: The Gospel Made Visible* (Nashville, TN: B&H, 2012), 69–77.

If you liked this book, you'll want to get involved in

Church Equip!

—

—

Do you have a desire to learn more about serving God through your local church?

Would you like to see how God can use you in new and exciting ways?

Get your church involved in Church Equip, an online ministry designed to prepare church leaders and church members to better serve God's mission and purpose.

Check us out at  **ChurchEquip.com**

CHURCH ANSWERS
FEATURING THOM RAINER

CP1749